IMAGES
of America

HERSHEY TRANSIT

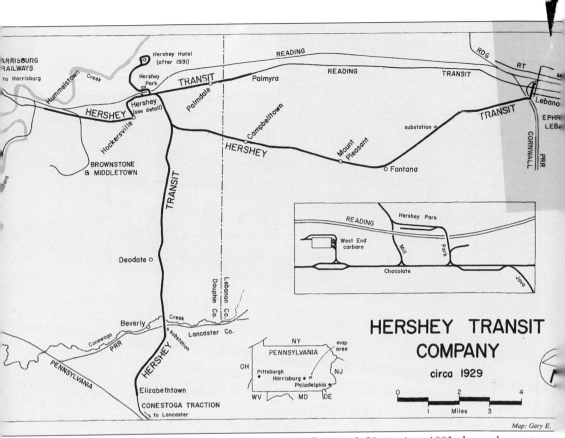

HERSHEY TRANSIT
COMPANY

circa 1929

0   2   4

Miles   3

Map: Gary E.

This c. 1929 map, originally published in *NRHS Bulletin*, vol. 58, no. 1, in 1993, shows the entire 35 miles of trackage for the Hershey Transit Company that included lines to Hummelstown, Campbelltown, Palmyra, Elizabethtown, Lebanon, and the Hotel Hershey loop. (Gary Kleinedler graphic/National Railway Historical Society.)

ON THE COVER: Traveling west on Chocolate Avenue is No. 7, built in 1914 by the Cincinnati Car Company. Traveling east is No. 20, a product of the J.G. Brill Company of Philadelphia. Both of these cars are carrying townspeople to and from the event occurring at the Community Center, which has attracted a great many of Hershey's citizens to its doors. Following the Brill car is No. 25, a box motor used to haul goods to customers along the line. This car may be making a delivery of materials to be used in the ongoing expansion of the Community Inn. This image captures the true significance the Hershey Transit Company had by providing vital connections throughout Hershey and the surrounding communities. (Neil Fasnacht collection.)

IMAGES
of America

HERSHEY TRANSIT

Friends of the Hershey Trolley
and the Hershey Derry Township
Historical Society

ARCADIA
PUBLISHING

Published by Arcadia Publishing
Charleston, South Carolina

Printed in the United States of America

Library of Congress Control Number: 2012947320

For all general information, please contact Arcadia Publishing:
Telephone 843-853-2070
Fax 843-853-0044
E-mail sales@arcadiapublishing.com
For customer service and orders:
Toll-Free 1-888-313-2665

Visit us on the Internet at www.arcadiapublishing.com

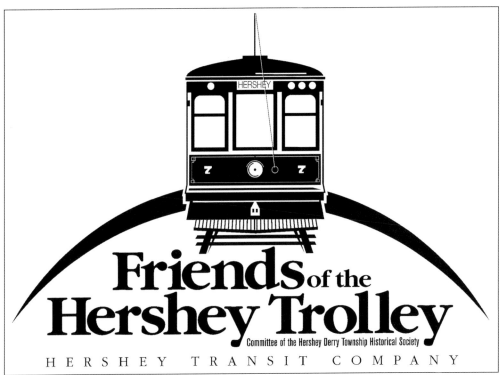

In 1995, Friends of the Hershey Trolley (FOHT), under the auspices of the Derry Township Historical Society, was formed with the mission of education and preservation of the Hershey Transit trolley system. Through the tireless efforts of many dedicated volunteers and with the assistance of other trolley preservation groups, FOHT has been able to locate and return to Hershey two of the cars that once ran along Chocolate Avenue. (Friends of the Hershey Trolley.)

CONTENTS

Acknowledgments 6

Introduction 7

1. The Early Years 9

2. Chocolate and Cocoa Avenues 15

3. The Hummelstown Line 43

4. The Campbelltown to Lebanon Line 55

5. The Barns 67

6. Milton Hershey School and the Trolleys 79

7. The Elizabethtown Line 87

8. The Hotel Line 101

9. Abandonment 113

10. Friends of the Hershey Trolley 123

ACKNOWLEDGMENTS

We are deeply grateful for the generous support and knowledge from many individuals and their contributions toward the creation of this book. Photograph collections from trolley enthusiasts Stan Bowman, Brad Ginder, Lisa Ginder, Andy Maginnis, Milton Hershey School, Don Rhoads Jr., and Chick Siebert as well as from the Neil Fasnacht collection, the Electric City Trolley Museum Association, and the Hershey Derry Township Historical Society were generously made available throughout this publication. All of the photographs in chapter 6 are courtesy of Milton Hershey School.

Special thanks go to volunteers and Friends of the Hershey Trolley, Susan Alger and the Milton Hershey School Department of History, Millie Landis, Neil Fasnacht, Brad Ginder, Bob Lawless, Don Rhoads Jr., and Lisa Schirato for their writing contributions and knowledge of the Hershey Transit System. We would like to recognize the Hershey Community Archives, the National Railway Historical Society, Lauren Fasnacht, Rockhill Trolley Museum (aka Railways to Yesterday, Inc.), Baltimore Streetcar Museum, Hershey Entertainment & Resorts, and the Free Library of Philadelphia for their invaluable contributions, without which this book would not have been possible. Historic references enabled us to clarify and confirm many different aspects of the Hershey Transit Company, these works include *Hershey Transit* by Benson W. Rohrbeck, *Chocolate Town Trolleys* by Richard H. Steinmetz, *Early Electric Cars of Baltimore* by Harold E. Cox, and *Trolleys of the Pennsylvania Dutch Country* by John D. Denney Jr.

If it were not for the foresight of Brad and Lisa Ginder and their interest and passion to locate the last remains of Hershey streetcars, Friends of the Hershey Trolley would never have come to fruition.

We also would like to remember a special friend, the late Tod Prowell, who credited his love of trolleys from riding on the Hershey streetcars as a young man. Tod dreamed of seeing streetcars operate once again in Hershey, and, just maybe, his dream will someday become reality.

INTRODUCTION

Trolleys and automobiles once shared the streets in Hershey, Pennsylvania. This is the story of how a transportation system formed, out of necessity and love for the people of Derry Township, and brought the local and surrounding communities together. Milton S. Hershey cared as much about the people in his town as he did about making chocolate. In the course of Hershey Transit Company's 42-year operation, from 1904 to 1946, the community was transported on 35 miles of track and a total of 34 streetcars, two of which have been preserved for future generations to appreciate.

The dark-green-and-cream-colored streetcars carried passengers and freight, most notably milk for the production of milk chocolate, starting in 1903 with the formation of the Hummelstown & Campbellstown Street Railway. Three J.G. Brill trolley cars were ordered from Philadelphia on February 5, 1904—one straight passenger and two combination freight-and-passenger cars. On October 15, 1904, the first streetcar left Hummelstown for Derry Church. Sponsored by Milton Hershey, trolley service was established from Derry Church to Palmyra by May 1905. In 1906, the village of Derry Church was renamed Hershey. Trolleys began running to Campbelltown during January 1908, and the line was extended to Lebanon on February 7, 1913. Passenger, freight, and express service between Hershey and Elizabethtown commenced on December 1, 1915. Many locals remember fondly the Hotel Hershey Loop, and you frequently hear reflection that the town officials should have at least saved this line.

Additional streetcars were added to the transit system in 1907 to accommodate the increased number of passengers and freight, and new trolleys lines emerged to extend service in outlying communities—Deodate & Hershey Street Railway, Elizabethtown & Deodate Street Railway, and the Lebanon & Campbellstown Street Railway. December 13, 1913, saw the formation of the Hershey Transit Company and the merging of surrounding streetcar subsidiaries into one, increasing the capacity of this "best-in-class" transportation system.

The 1920s saw the peak of the transit system, with not only regular passenger and freight service, but "picnic trolleys" or "specials" becoming common in Hershey and running as late as the 1930s. Streetcars from Lebanon, Lancaster, and Harrisburg were permitted on Hershey's lines and chartered by large groups for these specials events, such as a company picnic to Hershey Park. On occasion, a basket car was chartered to pick up and deliver family meals for these special excursions. For park visitors arriving on regular trolleys, a small single-truck trolley car was made available, free of charge, during the hours that the park was open, providing back-and-forth service between the square and Hershey Park.

Chick Siebert, trolley enthusiast and well-known trolley modeler, recalls his memories of riding Hershey Transit in the 1920s and 1930s in a letter dated May 2012:

> Back in the 1920s our annual family picnics at Hershey Park were probably a bit unusual. My dad was an environmental engineer (they called them sanitary engineers then) for

the Pennsylvania Department of Health. Because of this, he knew of the water reservoir on the hill above the park, now the site of the Hotel Hershey. The trolley line up the hill had been built some years before, but was not being used. There were a few tables up there, and that is where we had our picnic lunch before attacking the amusements in the park. Back then you paid for what you rode on, not an all day fee as it is now.

The 1939 trolley fan excursion on Hershey Transit was a successful occasion. The Elizabethtown and Lebanon lines were still operating and we rode both of them. The trip managers wanted to take the Birney No. 30 up the hill, but was a pretty hot day and the motorman was afraid that sun kinks in the rail might cause derailment of the single truck car. The superintendent, who was riding with us, motored the car up the hill, and it didn't derail.

Back around the same time period, Harrisburg Railways advertised a special trip to Hershey. Harrisburg Railways ran two cars to Hummelstown, where we connected with just one Hershey car. Boy, was that a jam-packed ride to Hershey. When we arrived at Hershey, most of the passengers went to the park, but I didn't. One of the three cars that Hershey Transit obtained from the Ephrata & Lebanon had just been re-worked, and was running on the hill line. So I rode up the hill on No4 or No7, I'm not sure which one it was.

Years later, when I was following in my dads foot steps as an environmental engineer, I had business with one of the Hershey Estates vice presidents about matters of stream pollution by the chocolate factory. At the end of the pollution business, I mentioned the Hershey Transit Co. The vice president said, "We should have saved the hill line."

If it had not been for World War II, Hershey Transit would have ended service by the end of 1942. Orders for buses and trucks had been placed, but rubber and gasoline were needed to support the war, and the Office of Defense Transportation ordered the dark green streetcars to stay in operation.

Today, there are few people in Derry Township that remember riding the beautiful green streetcars. Carl E. Stump of Hershey recalls his childhood memories about riding the trolley from Palmdale, one of many neighborhoods in Derry Township and located along Route 422 adjacent to Palmyra:

Students living west of Lingle Avenue in Derry Township could ride the trolley to and from the Hershey Public School at no expense. An extra trolley would come to Lingle Avenue each morning about 8 a.m. and start west, stopping at about six locations to pick up students. They also made a stop on Baums's Hill (current site of Hampton Inn) for students living in that area.

Two tickets for students to use for these rides were distributed at the end of each day by homeroom teachers, one to ride home and one to return the next day. No special trolley was provided at the end of the day and students rode on regularly scheduled runs between 3 and 5 p.m. If for some reason you arrived after 5 p.m. you had to get your ticket stamped in the transit office (in the Cocoa Inn) to ride home. While I speak only about my experiences from Palmdale, I believe the same service was provided for students living near the trolley routes to Elizabethtown and Hummelstown.

Most of these rides were calm and went smoothly. There were times, however, when "boys will be boys" behavior occurred. Some guys would wander to the rear platform and ring the bell or play with the sand release. This did not go over well with the conductor or motorman. Some of the men whose names I remember as Conductors and Motormen: Clem Miller, Harry King, Owen Hughes, Aaron Ebersole, and Dan Geib.

One

THE EARLY YEARS

While the Hershey Chocolate Factory was being constructed in his native Derry Church, Pennsylvania, Milton S. Hershey set out to establish an electric railway system. Its sole purpose was to transport the workforce needed for the factory's operation and transport supplies of fresh milk from the neighboring farms. The Hummelstown & Campbellstown Street Railway Company was organized on February 10, 1903, to connect a railway from Campbelltown, Lebanon County, Pennsylvania, to Hummelstown, Dauphin County, Pennsylvania. A charter was granted on March 13, 1903. Officers of the new company were Milton S. Hershey, president; John E. Snyder, Esq., secretary; and William H. "Lebbie" Lebkicher, treasurer.

With charter in hand, Milton S. Hershey hired Christian S. Maulfair (1840–1923), a real estate authority and auctioneer in the Lebanon Valley, who began the tedious task of negotiating land for the right-of-way. In May 1904, construction began on the line from Hockersville, Dauphin County, Pennsylvania, to Palmyra in Lebanon County, Pennsylvania. According to Ben Rohrbeck, a noted trolley historian, "The roadbed was graded by pick and shovel crews and horse-drawn dump carts. There was also a shortage of linemen and electricians to hang the overhead and install generating equipment during this early electric boom." He also indicated that securing the right-of-way was a slow process because some of the owners were against having new technology passing through their properties. But the challenges were soon overcome, and the first trolley left the corner of Second Street and North Railroad Avenue in Hummelstown, Pennsylvania, on October 15, 1904, and headed toward Derry Church, now Hershey. A report filed by the company to the Bureau of Railways, Department of Internal Affairs indicated that during its first year, from October to June 30, 1905, the system operated three trolleys and carried 115,801 passengers, generating revenue, including freight, of $5,995.74.

The Hummelstown & Campbellstown Street Railway would continue to grow within its original charter. In March 1905, the company issued $225,000 worth of securities to extend the railway to Campbelltown and on to Bismark (now Quentin), Pennsylvania. The latter was eventually abandoned. The line to Palmyra and the connection with the Lebanon & Annville Street Railway was eventually completed by May 1905. The line finally made it to Campbelltown in January 1908.

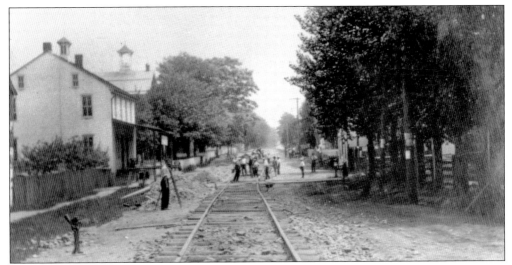

The Annville Journal reported on April 13, 1907, that the ties for the trolley line were deposited and that Campbelltown "will soon have an outlet to the great chocolate plant." In May 1907, the work on the line commenced. Above, workmen are laying tracks through the center of Campbelltown on the Horseshoe Pike near the former Campbelltown School, at far left. (Harvey S. Lineaweaver, Lebanon County Historical Society.)

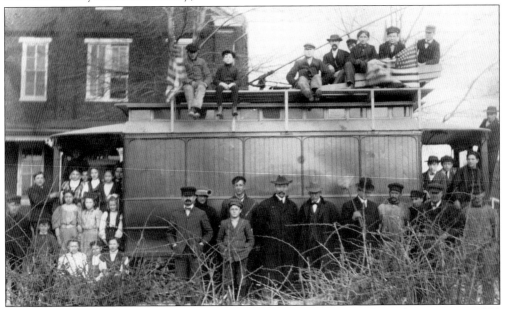

Photographed in front of the school in Campbelltown along the Horseshoe Pike in January 1908 are teacher Elmer E. Sloat and his students, local residents, and railway officials celebrating the arrival of the very first Hummelstown & Campbellstown Street Railway car. Included on this trip are Harry N. Herr (man holding a broom), chief engineer for the trolley line and Lebbie Lebkicher (standing to Herr's left), treasurer of the street railway. The work car pictured was originally built as a horsecar for use in Baltimore around 1890 and was later converted for electric operation. The Hummelstown & Campbellstown purchased the car in 1906 and converted it for use as a line car capable of installing and maintaining the overhead trolley wire system. (Harvey S. Lineaweaver, Don Rhoads Jr. collection.)

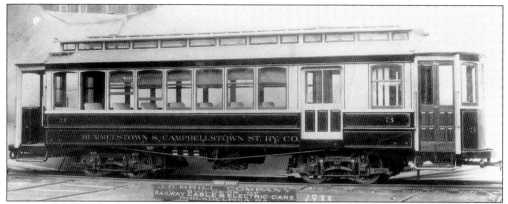

The J.G. Brill Company, organized in 1868, manufactured many of the cars operating on the Hershey Transit system and was an internationally known builder of street railway cars, among other forms of transportation equipment, over its lifetime as a company. No. 3 measured 41 feet long and was originally lettered for the Hummelstown & Campbellstown Street Railway upon its delivery on June 1, 1904. It was called a combination car because it carried both passengers and freight. (Brill Collection, Historical Society of Pennsylvania.)

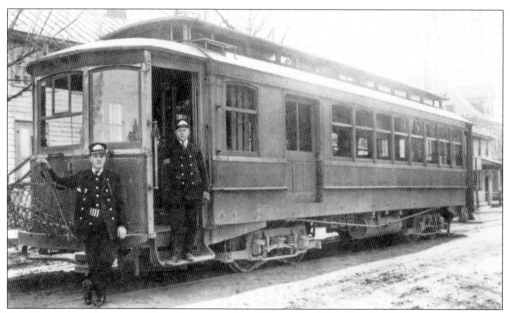

No. 2 was one of two combination cars ordered from Brill for Hershey Transit's predecessor, Hummelstown & Campbellstown Street Railway. Built exactly like No. 3, it arrived on June 1, 1904. The interior of the passenger compartment of both cars was finished in cherry wood. Fold-up seats were provided in the baggage compartment for the benefit of those who smoked. Here, the car is shown on the Berks and Dauphin Turnpike, now Route 422, in Palmyra, with motorman Harry "Whitey" Bistline on the right. (Neil Fasnacht collection.)

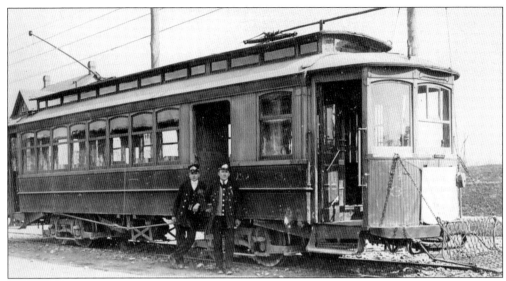

No. 3, photographed at an unidentified location in 1909, was constructed mostly of wood and had walk-over seats covered in rattan material. The term *walk-over* meant that the rider could adjust the seat depending on the direction the car was moving. Note the early cowcatcher made of rope and the canvas advertising sign attached to front, which reads, "Girls Wanted at Hershey Chocolate." No. 3 would eventually be changed into a full passenger car by the transit system's own workforce. (Neil Fasnacht collection.)

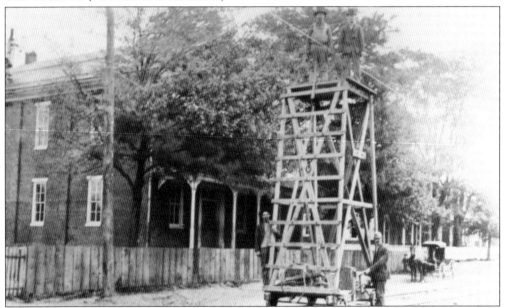

A Hummelstown & Campbellstown work crew adjusts the overhead wire in front of the school along the Horseshoe Pike in Campbelltown. Note the very early and more than likely homemade scaffold that was used on the wheels. This image was created by Harvey S. Lineaweaver (1893–1984), a Campbelltown resident who became interested in photography in his teen years, learning the trade from a well-known Lebanon photographer, Luther G. Harpel. Lineaweaver captured many of the town's happenings in the early to mid-20th century. (Harvey S. Lineaweaver, Lebanon County Historical Society.)

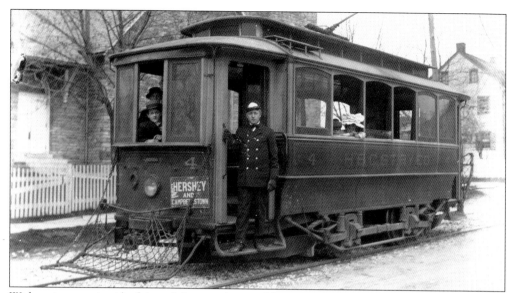

With an increase in ridership and the completion of the extension to Campbelltown, Hummelstown & Campbellstown No. 4 was purchased from Baltimore, Maryland, in 1906. A product of Brill, it was ordered in 1893 equipped with a 21-E truck containing two Westinghouse model 3 motors. The car with motorman Harry "Whitey" Bistline was photographed in Campbelltown in front of the Salem Reformed Church. This particular building was erected in 1897/1898 after a severe storm destroyed the previous church built in 1845. Today, it is Salem United Church of Christ. (Harvey S. Lineaweaver, Don Rhoads Jr. collection.)

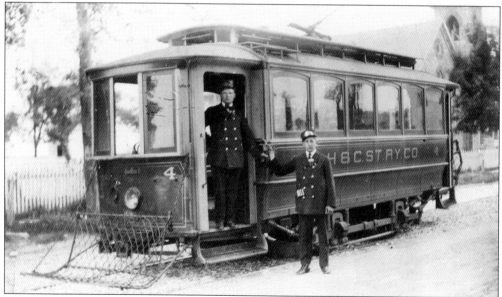

No. 4 and its crew, George Holzman (left) and Harry "Whitey" Bistline, are shown in Campbelltown. This 18-foot car was capable of carrying 28 passengers. With the single-truck cars, when a change in direction was required, the motorman would remove the retriever used for supplying tension to the trolley pole, and carry it to the other end of the car. Note the circular bracket on the front right of the headlight used to attach the retriever. No. 4 was eventually retired by the Hershey Transit Company in the early 1930s. (Harvey S. Lineaweaver, Don Rhoads Jr. collection.)

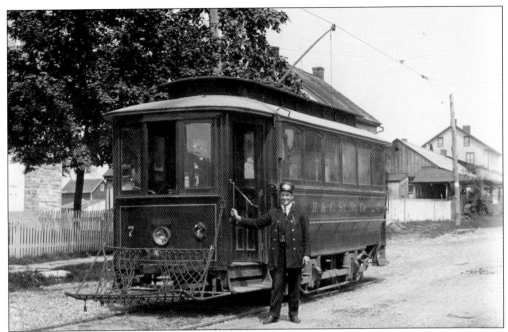

Motorman William "Bill" Harper smiles for the camera in front of No. 7 in Campbelltown. This 28-seat single-truck trolley rode upon a Peckham model 7-B truck and was part of a 52-car order from Brill in 1892. Constructed as a 15-foot, 10-inch cable car trailer, it was converted to electric operation in 1897. It was purchased secondhand from Baltimore, Maryland, in 1910 and was retired by Hershey Transit in 1934. (Harvey S. Lineaweaver, Don Rhoads Jr. collection.)

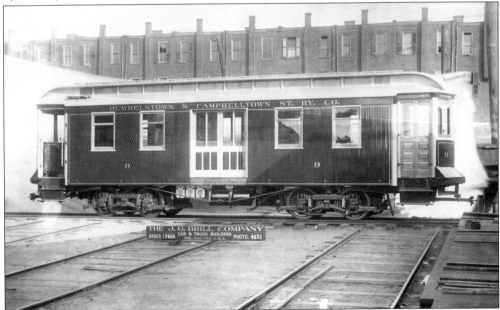

Express car No. 9 arrived from Brill on the trolley line in May 1911. According to the *Hershey Press*, Hershey's local newspaper, on May 11, 1911, the car was "purchased principally for the transportation of milk, but is so arranged as to be turned into a passenger coach in a few moment's time." This car operated until about 1931. (Neil Fasnacht collection.)

Two

Chocolate and Cocoa Avenues

The southwest corner of Cocoa and Chocolate Avenues was once home to Hershey's Community Inn and the offices for the Hershey Transit Company. Across the street from the Community Inn, an island in the middle of Chocolate Avenue, lined with park benches, served as a waiting room and Hershey Transit's main interchange station.

Hershey was just like any small town in America, with its post office, volunteer fire company, drugstore, green grocer, and department store, except for one thing: it had its very own chocolate factory. Downtown Hershey, in the 1920s, was a bustling center filled with people, the aroma of chocolate in the air, and streetcars everywhere.

Cars built by the J.G. Brill Company were most popular in Hershey, but there were other favorites, such as the beautiful Ephrata & Lebanon Traction Company cars purchased for their ability to climb the hill to Hotel Hershey and Senior Hall. During the very early years, single-truck cars were purchased from Baltimore to address the needs of providing increased service and the rising popularity of Hershey Park.

No. 1, No. 2, and No. 3—one straight passenger and two combines—were Milton Hershey's first purchase in 1903 from the J.G. Brill Company.

Chick Siebert recalls Hershey's Brill semi-convertible cars:

Although the arch roof Hershey cars were typical Brill semi-convertibles (with extra low window sills), the end windows were not the standard Brill design, if there was a standard. Most Brill semi-convertibles had a wider center window, presumably for visibility, but the Hershey cars had three windows of equal width. This is just one example of the variation in details that could be obtained on Brill semi-convertible cars. The deck roof double truck cars, No1, No2, No3, and No6, had typical and more usual end window details; a wider center window flanked by narrower side windows. There were 12 of the Brill arch roof semi-convertibles: No10, No11, No16, No17, No18, No19, No20, No21, No22, No23, No26, and No27.

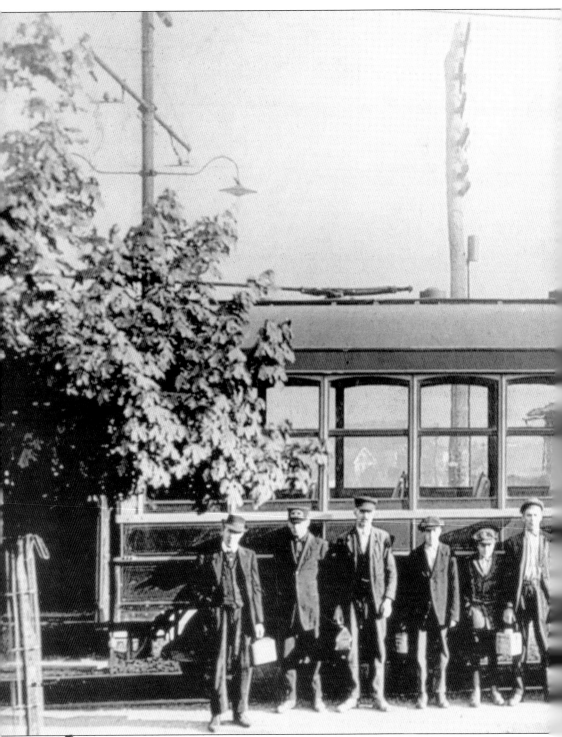

Captured here traveling west on East Chocolate Avenue in front of the Cocoa House is No. 1.
Built by the J.G. Brill Company, of Philadelphia, for the Hummelstown & Campbellstown Street
Railway in 1903, No. 1 was one of the most-photographed Hershey Transit trolleys and a favorite of

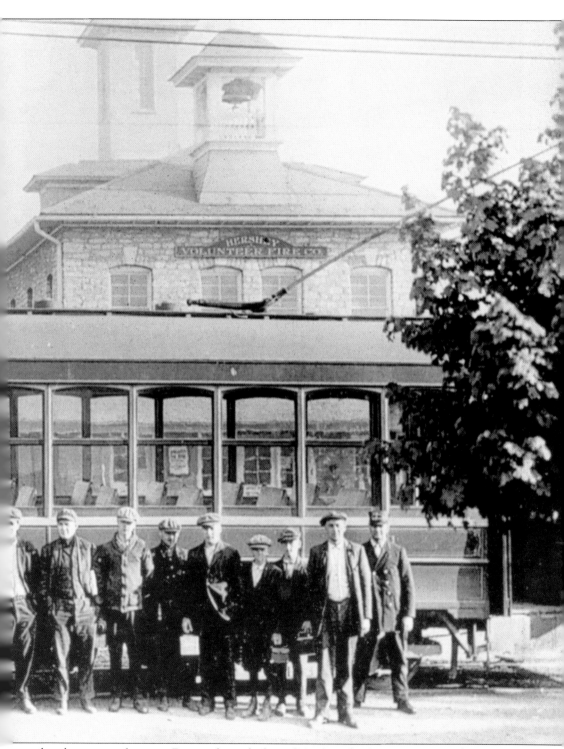

rail enthusiasts on fan trips. During the early days of Hershey, the Cocoa House was home to the Hershey Volunteer Fire Company, post office, and general store. Hershey Transit motormen and line workers, some with their lunch pails, pose for the photographer. (Neil Fasnacht collection.)

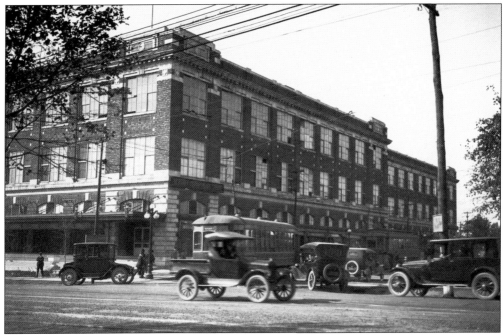

Pictured is an early street scene in Hershey, looking north past the Hershey Department Store. The store, originally the Hershey Press Building, was constructed in 1916. It not only held the printing company, but also Hershey Laundry and worship services for St. Joan of Arc Catholic Church. The Hershey Department Store, originally located on the southwest corner of Chocolate and Cocoa Avenues, moved to the Hershey Press Building in 1920. (Milton Hershey School.)

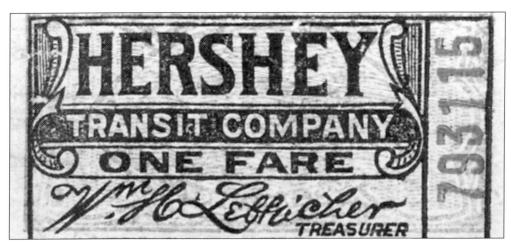

William Henry "Lebbie" Lebkicher, a close personal friend of Milton S. Hershey, signed this early "one fare" Hershey Transit ticket. Lebbie and Milton grew close during Milton's early start-up years in Philadelphia, Pennsylvania, and Lebbie followed Milton to Derry Church—later known as Hershey—where he held various positions in the chocolate company and town. (Neil Fasnacht collection.)

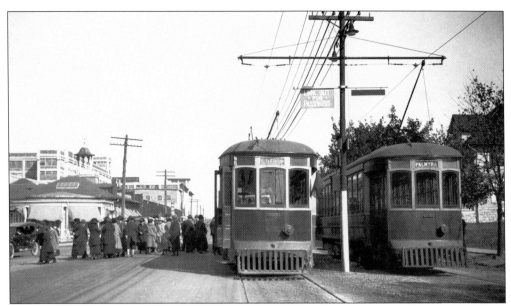

An early street scene on Chocolate Avenue features one trolley heading east to Palmyra and the other trolley returning from Elizabethtown. The Hershey Café, with its prominent awnings and cupola on the roof, is at left in the foreground, and the factory for the chocolate company in the background. The building for the Hershey Café was originally constructed as the first carbarn for the Hummelstown & Campbellstown Street Railway, later the Hershey Transit Company. (Milton Hershey School.)

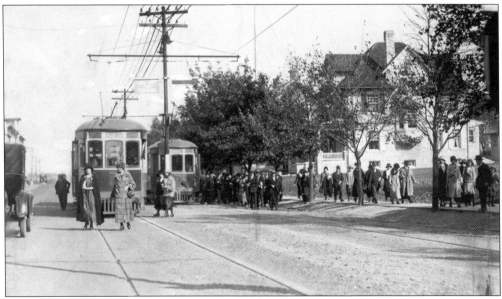

Chocolate Avenue was a central hub of activity in the town of Hershey and the main station for passengers. Looking east, two early streetcars manufactured by the J.G. Brill Company are seen, one with a "Special Car" sign prominent in the trolley's window. The rollsign was changeable and allowed the motorman to display the car's destination for the benefit of boarding passengers. Most likely, the passengers are going to a special event or Sunday church services, judging by their attire. (Milton Hershey School.)

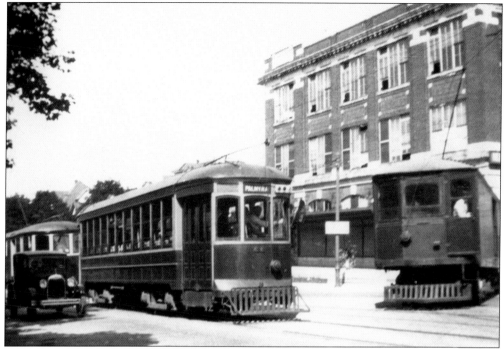

Two streetcars produced by the J.G. Brill Company of Philadelphia—No. 20, a straight passenger car in 1915, and No. 29, the freight express in 1914—maneuver through downtown Hershey on Chocolate Avenue in front of the Hershey Department Store. No. 20 and No. 29 ran for Hershey Transit until the end of operations in 1946. (Neil Fasnacht collection.)

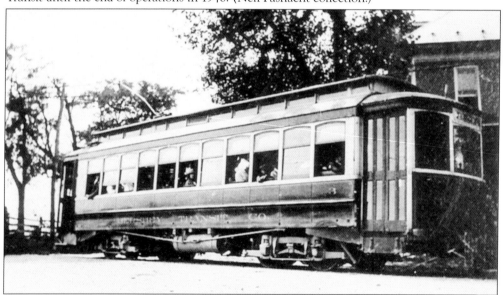

In this rare photograph, No. 3 is pictured as a passenger car at Erb's Grocery Store at the intersection of Route 322 and Hockersville Road; it was travelling north towards Chocolate Avenue. Purchased in 1903 as a combination car, it was used to carry passengers and freight. Sometime after 1913, Hershey Transit converted it into a straight passenger car, possibly after freight motors No. 24 and No. 25 were placed in service. (Brad Ginder collection.)

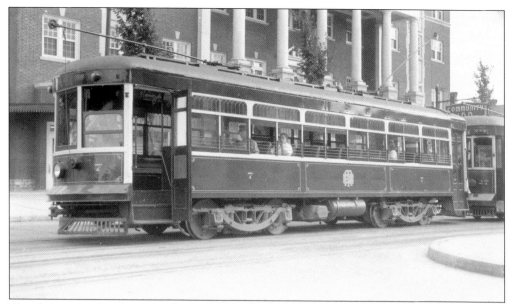

The Community Inn, known in later years as the Cocoa Inn, was located on the southwest corner of Chocolate and Cocoa Avenues. It not only had accommodations and restaurant services, such as the famous Oyster Bar, but it also housed the offices for the Hershey Transit Company. Chick Siebert photographed No. 7 with No. 27 behind it on July 16, 1939, waiting for passengers before heading east on Chocolate Avenue. (Chick Siebert.)

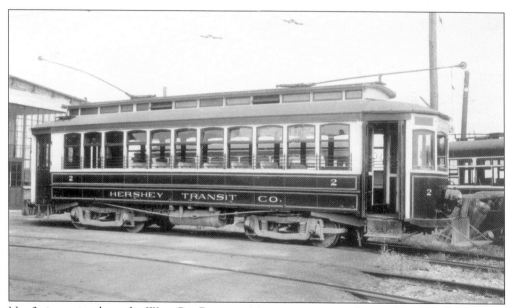

No. 2 sits patiently at the West Car Barn awaiting passengers on August 13, 1939, for a special trip of the National Railway Historical Society. Originally purchased as a combination car in 1903 from the J.G. Brill Company, No. 2 was identical to No. 3 and was also converted to a straight passenger car. It lasted on the Hershey Transit system until 1943. No. 1, No. 2, and No. 3 were all purchased as deck roof cars, 27-G1 trucks equipped with Westinghouse 68C motors and Westinghouse K-6 controls. (Chick Siebert.)

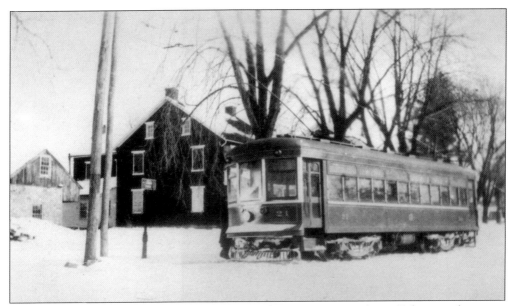

Ephrata & Lebanon Traction Company No. 21 is shown on a snowy day in Ephrata picking up a passenger. It was one of four cars delivered by the Cincinnati Car Company in 1915 to equip the line for interurban trolley service. A third coach and an additional combine had been ordered in 1914 by the E&L for a sister line located along the New Jersey coast, but the order for these cars was cancelled when the Trenton, Lakewood & Seacoast Railway was unable to complete the line due to wartime material shortages and franchise issues. (Lisa Schirato collection.)

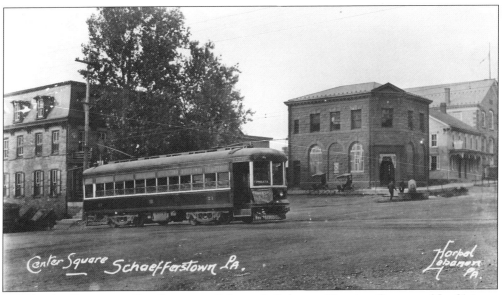

Built by the Cincinnati Car Company, Ephrata & Lebanon Traction Company No. 21 is on the square in Schaefferstown, Purchased secondhand by Hershey Transit in 1933, square in Schaefferstown. Purchased secondhand by Hershey Transit in 1933 and would become No. 7, it was converted, along with two of its sisters (one straight passenger and one combine), for double-ended operations. Additional modifications were made to the combine to convert it to a straight passenger car. (Andy Maginnis collection.)

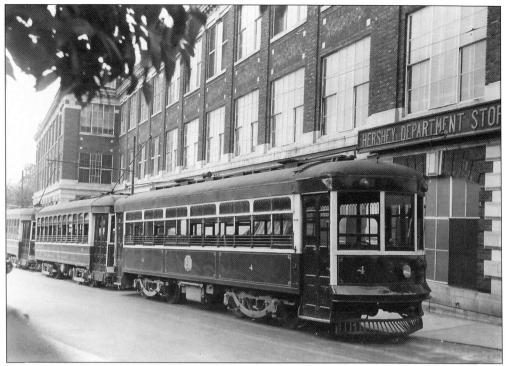

No. 4, one of Hershey's three streetcars purchased from the Lancaster, Ephrata & Lebanon Street Railway in 1933 and geared to climb mountainous terrain, sits idle next to the green grocer, later an Acme store, located in the back of the Hershey Department Store building on August 13, 1939. These cars were lined up on Sunday morning while the boys from Hershey Industrial School attended church services in the Hershey Theatre. (Andy Maginnis collection.)

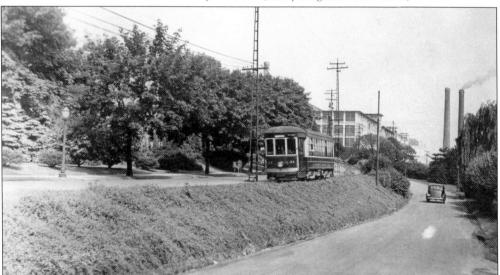

No. 21 heads south on Java Avenue in Hershey toward Homestead Road and the junction that continues on to Campbelltown, Lebanon, or Elizabethtown. Many of the streets in Hershey, such as Java, Caracas, Bahia, and Trinidad Avenues, are named for areas or countries where cocoa beans are grown for use in the production of chocolate. (Neil Fasnacht collection.)

HERSHEY TRANSIT COMPANY

Conductor's and Motorman's Daily Report of
Condition of Car No.................................

....19 ....

Car taken from..M.

Car { Returned to
{ Delivered to..M.

Mark ✕ after parts of car which need repairs.
Details not mentioned can be noted in remarks column.

Air Brake Compressor .	....	Heater Switch	....
Air Pipe Leaking . . .	....	Hot Journals	....
Air Valve (Eng.) . . .	....	Jack and Handle	....
Air Valve (Whistle) .	....	Light Circuit (Bat.) . .	....
Axles	....	Markers	....
Battery	....	Light Circuit (Car) . .	....
Bell	....	Motor No.	....
Bell Cord	....	Register	....
Bearings	....	Register Cord	....
Brakes	....	Retriever	....
Brake Riggings	....	Resistance	....
Broom	....	Relays	....
Bucking	....	Sand	....
Cables	....	Sanders	....
Canopy Switches . . .	....	Seats	....
Charged	....	Signs	....
Controller	....	Sign Lights	....
Curtains	....	Springs	....
Draw Bar	....	Steps	....
Doors	....	Switches or Fuses . . .	....
Fenders	....	Trolley Cord	....
Flag	....	Trolley Poles	....
Floor	....	Trolley Stands	....
Gears and Casings . . .	....	Trolley Wheels	....
Grab Handles	....	Windows	....
Gongs	....	Wheels (Car)	....
Headlight	....	Whistles	....

REMARKS:

_____

_____

NOTICE: This report must be properly filled out for every car turned into car-barn, signed by Conductor and Motorman, and turned in at car-barn or handed to Foreman in charge.

_____ *Conductor*

_____ *Motorman*

Master Mechanic will certify repairs made and turn this
report over to the Superintendent.

Repairs made...193........

M. M.

5M-5-9-41-Ⓑ

Daily reporting of the streetcar's condition was an important task completed by the conductor or motorman. This 1930s list shows all of the hardware on the trolley that needed to be checked; Hershey Transit Company employees documented any repair needs when the car was returned to the barn. The primary responsibility of the motorman and conductor was safety. Most cars would have one motorman and one conductor. The motorman's responsibilities were to operate the car, verify the position of track switches before crossing, operate the bell at all crossings, and put the trolley away at the end of the shift. The conductor was responsible for collecting and counting fares, overseeing the safety of passengers, signaling stops, making sure passengers were seated before the trolley began to move, ringing the signal twice, making sure the doors were closed, and answering passenger questions. (Milton Hershey School.)

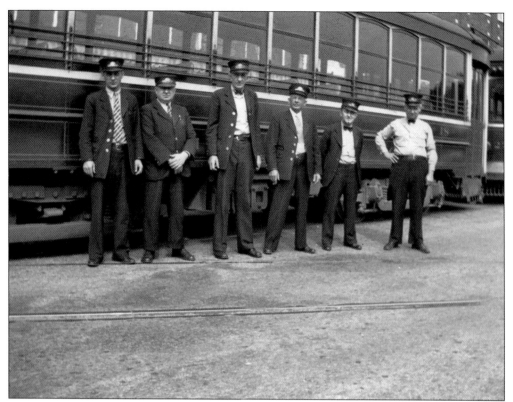

Motormen and conductors pose with No. 18 on the Hershey Department Store siding. Interviewed on September 3, 1955, retired superintendent of the Hershey Transit Company, A.W. Flowers, stated, "Hershey was very proud of the Transit Company. He always wanted the cars in good condition. He was sorry to see the transit line go. He was not alive when we abandoned the line, but he knew it was coming." (Neil Fasnacht collection.)

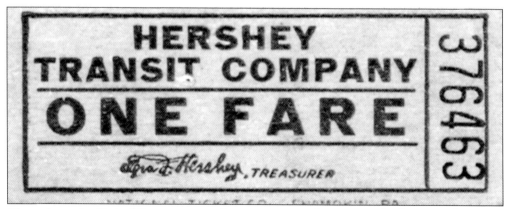

Throughout the United States, street railway systems used a variety of ticketing styles. Many systems used a token or coin-like piece for calculating ridership. Hershey Transit used paper tickets throughout its history. Pictured here is a Hershey Transit "one fare" ticket, produced by the National Ticket Company located in Shamokin. National Ticket is a family-owned company that has been operating in Pennsylvania for over 100 years. (Milton Hershey School.)

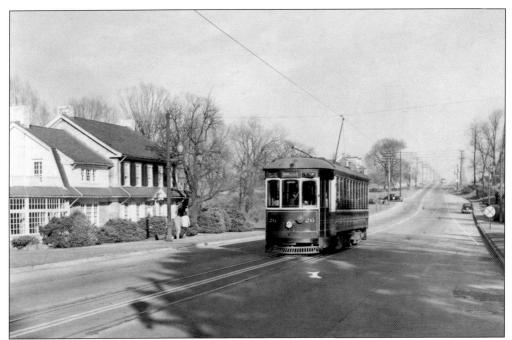

Bound for Hummelstown, No. 26 is seen passing the Teahouse, located on East Chocolate Avenue. Opening on September 1, 1922, the Teahouse, formerly a farmhouse, was an endearing favorite establishment among the residents of Hershey. Following the severe flooding that occurred in 1972, the beautiful limestone building was razed, against the objections of the local residents. (Neil Fasnacht collection.)

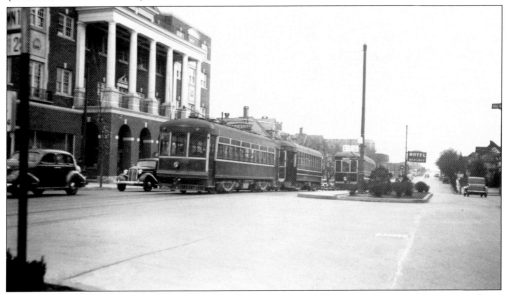

Photographed here on March 27, 1938, is the waiting area for customers traveling west from Hershey. Chocolate Avenue was widened for two blocks in the center of town to accommodate both streetcar and automobile traffic. Eastbound passengers waited on the sidewalk in front of the Community Inn. During inclement weather, passengers would wait inside the Community Inn. (Stan Bowman Jr. collection.)

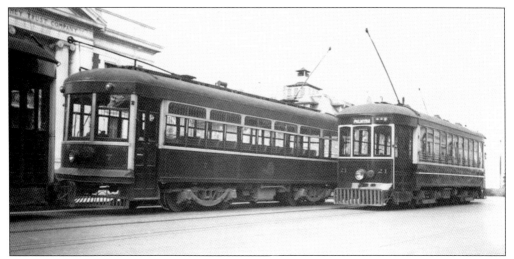

No. 7 travels west in front of the Hershey Trust Company building on Chocolate Avenue, while No. 21 heads east toward Palmyra on March 27, 1938. Connecting trolley service between Palmyra and Myerstown was provided by the Reading Street Railway Company. This service was discontinued on July 21, 1930, when the line was shuttered due to nonpayment of back taxes. (Stan Bowman Jr. collection.)

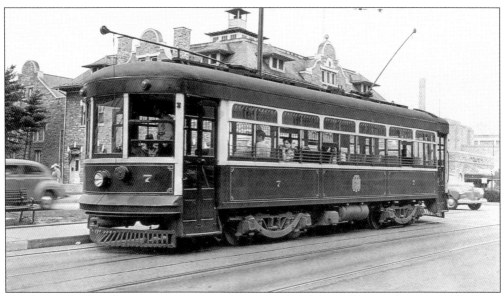

No. 7 is stopped at the main passenger terminal for the Hershey Transit Company. The large limestone structure behind No. 7 was the Cocoa House, built in 1905. It held a number of town establishments and organizations throughout its lifetime and was razed in 1963. During the early years, the Cocoa House was home to the town's post office, general store, volunteer fire company, and bank. After 1910, the building was renovated for use as the first Hershey Public Library, the YMCA, and the YWCA, until these activities were moved to the Community Building across the street, just before the Cocoa House was demolished. Note the siren tower atop the Cocoa House to warn the town of a fire. It was also used during the war as an air-raid siren. (Stan Bowman Jr. collection.)

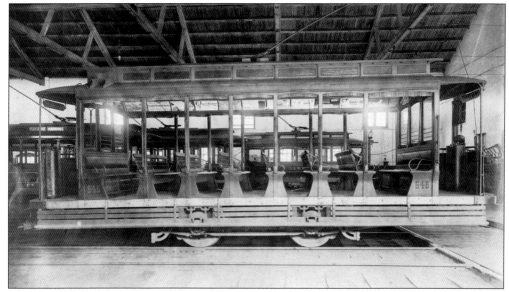

To bring patrons from the square in town to Hershey Park, Hershey Transit purchased two 8-bench open cars from the Philadelphia Rapid Transit Company, similar to No. 646. Built in 1894 by the Laclede Car Company of St. Louis for the Philadelphia Traction Company, the cars had a seating capacity of 40. Shipped from Philadelphia on July 1, 1912, upon arrival the cars were repainted and renumbered as No. 12 and No. 14. Hershey Transit never had a car numbered 13, as it was considered to be unlucky. (Free Library of Philadelphia, Print and Picture Collection.)

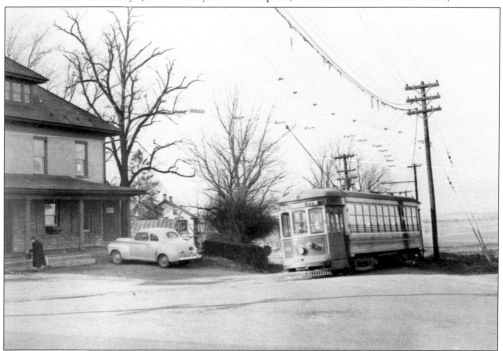

Heading north on Hockersville Road, No. 26 is turning off present-day Route 322 on its way from Hummelstown. Pictured in the background is Erb's Grocery Store, a local fixture of the community. (Neil Fasnacht collection.)

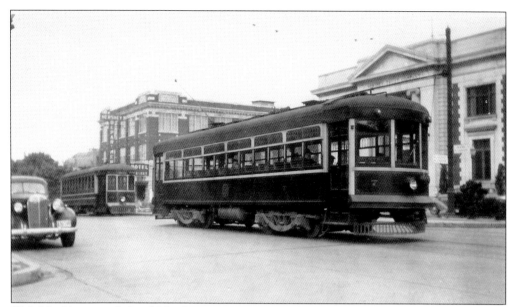

With No. 21 tagging behind, No. 7 moves east on Chocolate Avenue in front of the Hershey Trust Company building and toward Palmyra. Designed by well-known Lancaster architect C. Emlen Urban, the Hershey Trust Company building, at 1 West Chocolate Avenue, was constructed in 1914. The Hershey National Bank, established in 1925, was also located in the Hershey Trust Company building. (Neil Fasnacht collection.)

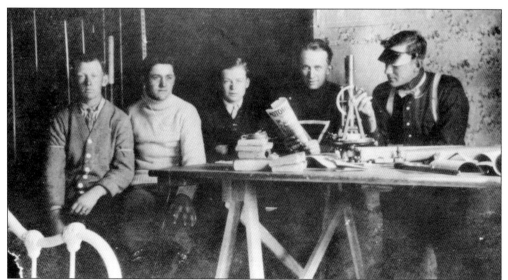

This 1912 photograph shows the surveyors that planned for both the Lebanon and Elizabethtown lines on the Hershey Transit system. Pictured, from left to right, are Artman Boyer, a Mr. Keller, Chas Miller, George Gerth, and Ira Hershey. (Chas K. Miller, Hershey Derry Township Historical Society.)

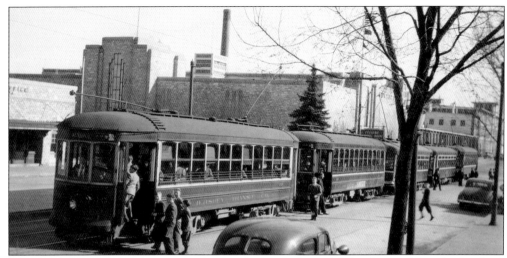

Hershey Transit served frequent runs for the Hershey Industrial School, to and from both school and church. Pictured are several streetcars on Chocolate Avenue in downtown Hershey. The cars are headed both east and west, as the boys lived in farmhouses spread throughout Derry Township. The old Hershey Post Office is at far left, with the chocolate factory behind and to the right. (Neil Fasnacht collection.)

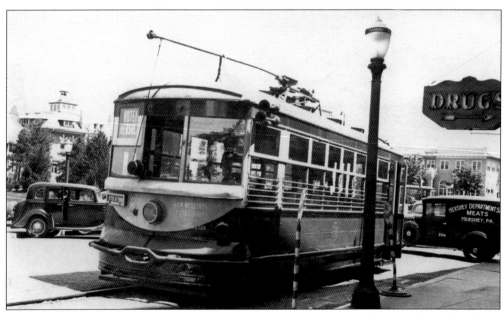

No. 30, a one-of-a-kind Birney car designed and produced in 1923 for the Grand Rapids Railway of Michigan, was purchased by Hershey Transit in 1936 for use on the Hotel Line. Just over 28 feet long, this single-truck car provided a very rough ride for passengers. Photographed here on the Hershey Department Store siding in 1936, it was later sold to Indiana Railways Company in Marion, where it ran until being retired in 1947. (Neil Fasnacht collection.)

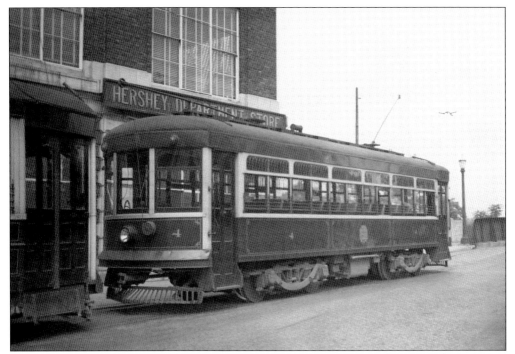

On June 23, 1940, No. 4, one of three cars purchased from the Lancaster, Ephrata & Lebanon Street Railway, waits on the Hershey Department Store siding on Park Avenue. In 1940, the Hershey Department Store had everything needed for the average household, including a pharmacy and green grocer. (Neil Fasnacht collection.)

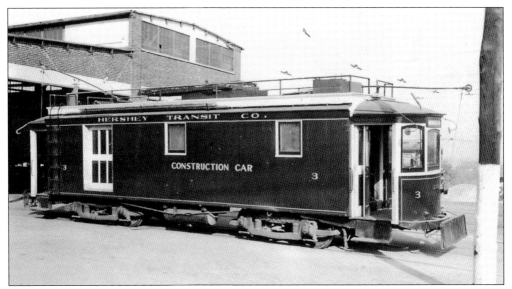

The West Car Barn was a busy location for the storage and maintenance of the Hershey Transit system. No. 3, as the work car, sits on the southernmost track in its usual location in the carbarn. (Al Gilcher, Andy Maginnis collection.)

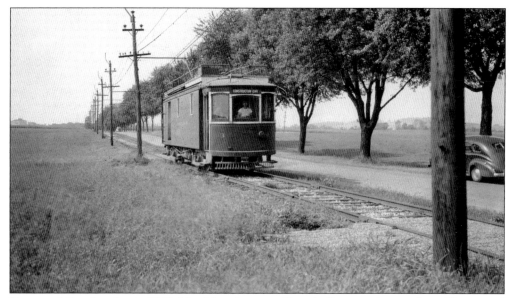

On a cool October day in 1946, No. 3 heads out to Campbelltown going south on Homestead Lane. (Neil Fasnacht collection.)

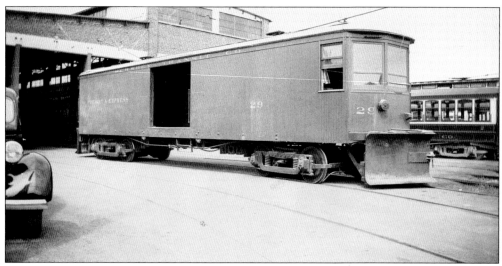

No. 29 was a wooden freight express car built by J.G. Brill Company in 1914 for the Pennsylvania & New Jersey Railway. Surplus when routes were abandoned, the car was purchased by Hershey Transit in 1920, and it traveled here under its own power. The snowplows seen here were previously used on work car No. 5. In later years, the car was modified to also perform duties as a line car. (Brad Ginder collection.)

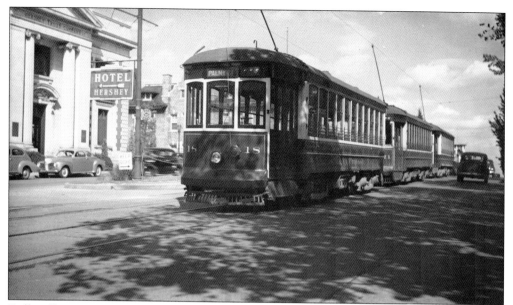

Brill trolleys No. 18 and No. 21 are lined up by the waiting room in front of the Community Inn ready to head east on Chocolate Avenue toward Palmyra. The Hotel Hershey sign stood for many years in the square of Hershey. The Hotel Hershey remains a popular destination for not only visitors, but also local residents. (Hershey Derry Township Historical Society Collection.)

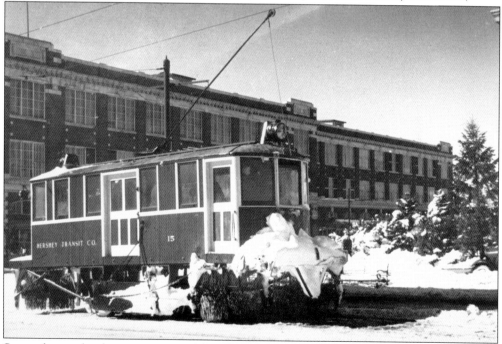

Stopped near the department store, No. 15 waits for its crew to return from a break. Ordered by the Hummelstown & Campbellstown on August 23, 1912, this sweeper was part of a stock run of half a dozen long-broom sweepers built by J.G. Brill to have on hand to be able to quickly meet customers' demands. It kept the streets free of snow until 1946, when it was retired. (Neil Fasnacht collection.)

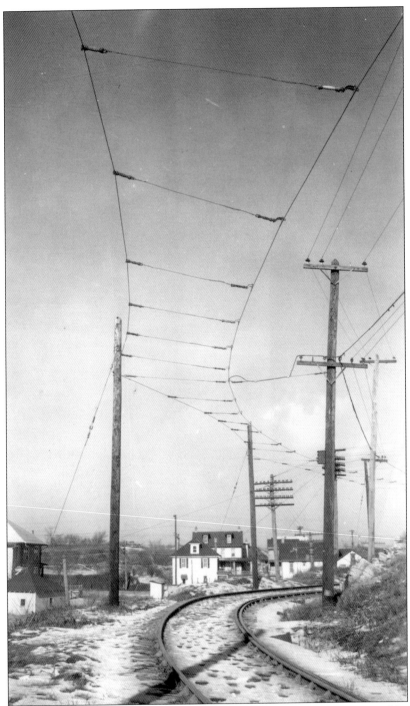

Photographed on January 21, 1941, is the right-of-way in the Swatara Station neighborhood of Hershey. This neighborhood was home to many Italian immigrants who settled in Derry Church and worked in the limestone quarries and in the chocolate factory. Clearly shown is the intricate support system required to keep the overhead wire aligned with the track along areas of sharp curves. (Chick Siebert.)

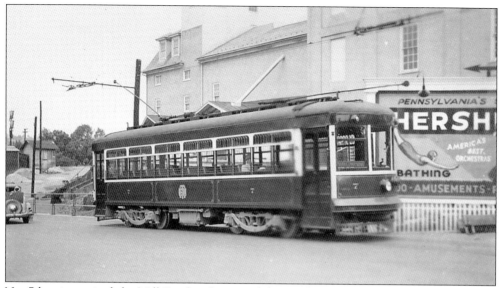

No. 7 has just exited the Mill Road underpass of the Reading Railroad. It is preparing to turn onto Chocolate Avenue., most likely heading for the Hershey waiting room. The building on the right is the implement shop owned by the Hershey Farm Company. Note the unusual lead-window design featured on the Cincinnati cars and the billboard advertising Hershey leisure activities. (Neil Fasnacht collection.)

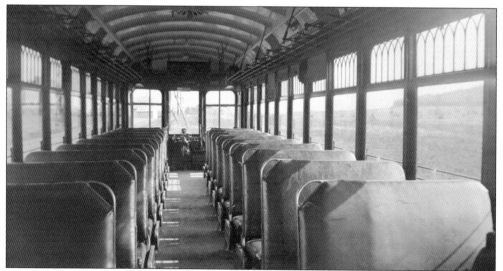

This view of No. 4 shows the brass luggage rack and the leather walk-over seats. When built, the car was equipped with the latest innovation of the day: telephones. These phones were used to talk with the dispatcher via wayside communication connections located at regular intervals along the route. (Hershey Derry Township Historical Society.)

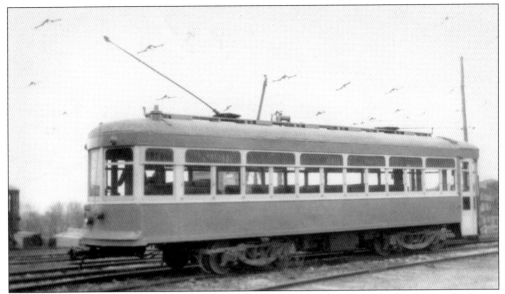

A unique March 1933 photograph shows Lancaster, Ephrata & Lebanon No. 21 shortly after being delivered to Hershey Transit at the West Car Barn. The car is in its original configuration prior to altering the door configuration from three to four doors and conversion from a single-end car to a double-ended car. This streetcar would be renumbered by Hershey Transit as No. 7. (Lisa Schirato collection.)

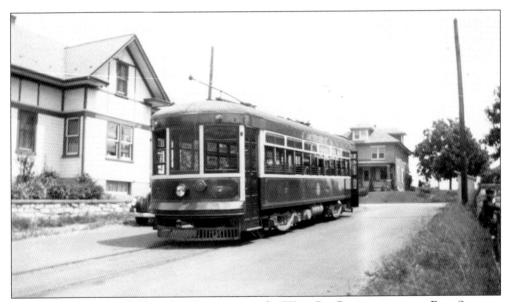

No. 7 headed north off Chocolate Avenue into the West Car Barn property on First Street, a popular location for railfans to photograph the streetcars of the Hershey Transit system. (Stan Bowman Jr. collection.)

36

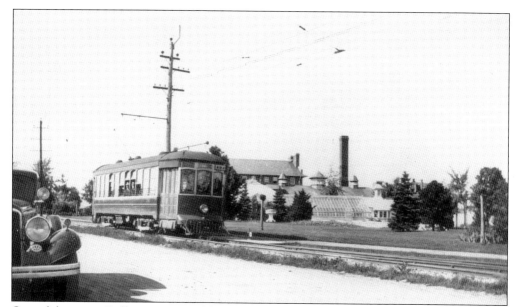

One of the many Brill semi-convertible cars, No. 26 heads to Campbelltown along present-day Route 322 in front of the old Hershey Industrial School property in Hershey. In this view, one can see how the windows recess into the arched roof of the trolley car. (Dick Steinmetz, Chick Siebert collection.)

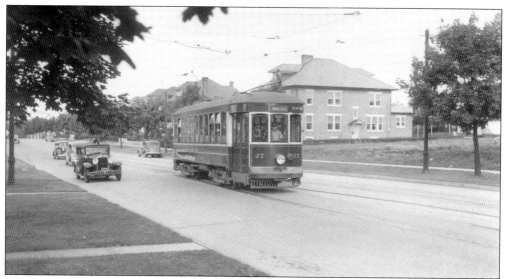

No. 27 was purchased along with No. 26 from the J.G. Brill Company in March 1920 and equipped with Brill 27MCB1 trucks and Westinghouse 632 motors. Chick Siebert photographed No. 27 on a bright summer day, July 16, 1939, heading west on Chocolate Avenue. This car operated the last trip to Elizabethtown on the evening of June 23, 1940. (Chick Siebert.)

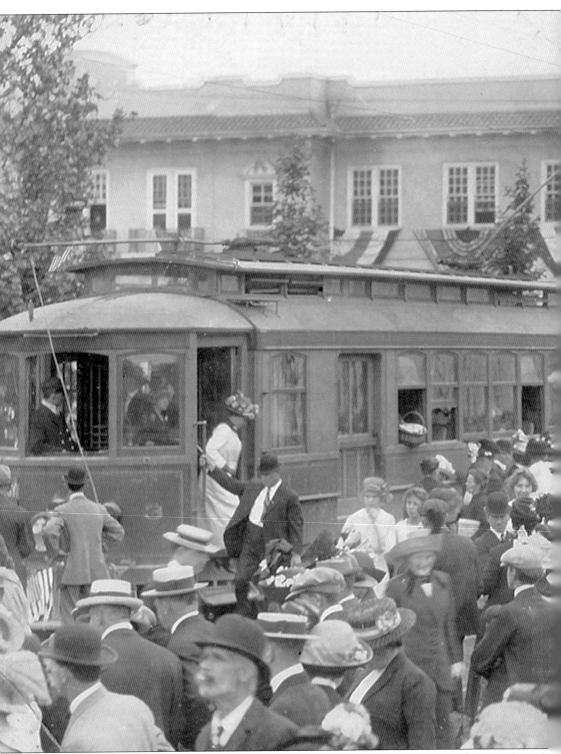

During the year 1913, the town of Hershey celebrated its 10th anniversary with a parade and other festivities. No. 3, one of the first three streetcars purchased by Milton S. Hershey for the

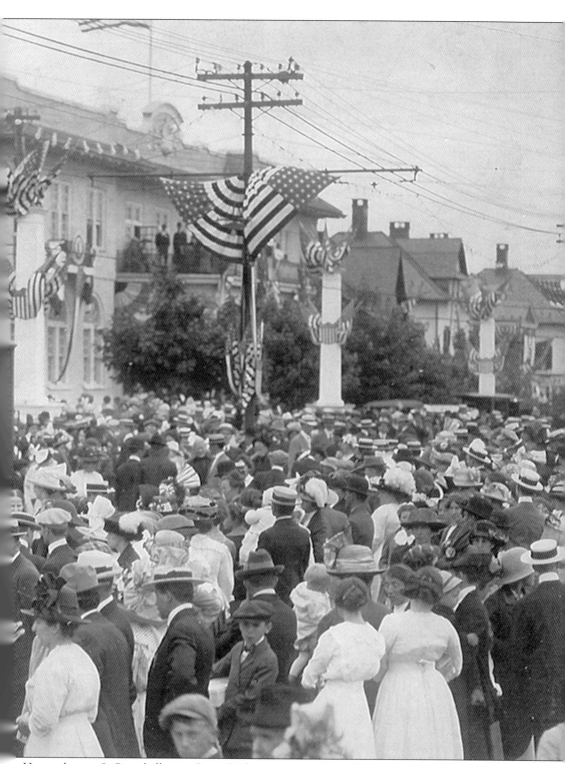

Hummelstown & Campbellstown Street Railway system, is shown here in its original configuration as a combine and is busy bringing people to the day's celebration. (Lisa Schirato collection.)

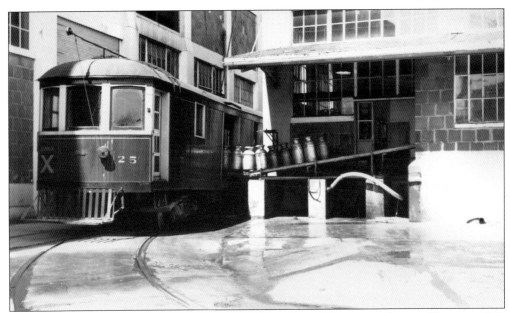

Daily deliveries of milk were essential to keep the factory in continuous production. To accomplish this, Hershey Transit made six round-trips each day between the Lebanon and Elizabethtown lines, traveling as far as Lincoln and Mount Joy to receive milk from the surrounding farms. Starting in 1904 with one dairy farm with 35 cows, the company owned and operated two dozen dairy farms with nearly two thousand head of livestock a decade later. (Neil Fasnacht collection.)

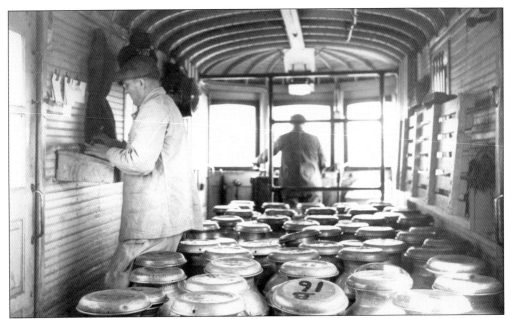

This view of freight motor No. 25 reveals details not often seen. The car was designed by James K. Putt and was constructed under his supervision in 1917 by the Hershey Transit Company. By constructing its own equipment, Hershey Transit found that cars could be built quicker, stronger, and cheaper than ordering from a builder. The 40-foot-long car had a capacity of 10 tons and was used daily to carry milk shipments. (Neil Fasnacht collection.)

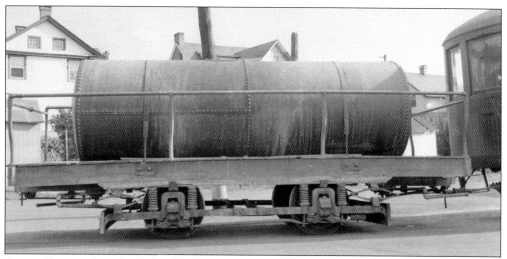

Originally one of two Laclede 8-bench open cars purchased from Philadelphia Rapid Transit in July 1912, No. 12 was used to shuttle people between the square in Hershey and Hershey Park. As attendance rose and new equipment was purchased, the usefulness of this car was limited. There was, however, a growing demand to transport more milk to the factory, and the car was converted for use as a 3,000-gallon insulated tank car. Typically used between Hershey and the off-line milk station located in Lincoln, No. 12 was retired in 1929, when the milk contract with the Lancaster, Ephrata & Lebanon Street Railway was cancelled. (Neil Fasnacht collection.)

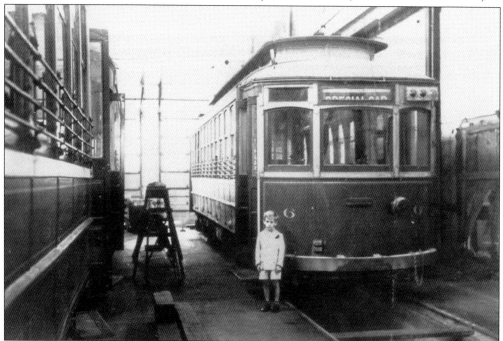

Purchased for the Hummelstown and Campbelltown Street Railway Company on January 12, 1910, No. 6 was manufactured by the J.G. Brill Company, equipped with Brill 27G trucks and Westinghouse 101 motors. Rarely photographed, this deck-roof wooden car is seen here at the west end in the West Car Barn, at an unknown date. No. 6 ran on revenue service until 1942. (Neil Fasnacht collection.)

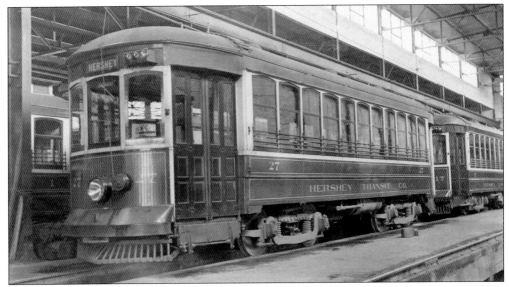

Two of the popular Brill semi-convertible cars, No. 27 and No. 17 wait for their turns at revenue service in the West Car Barn in Hershey. Both cars had a seating capacity of 44 passengers and ran in service until the end of operations in December 1946. (Russell Koons, Hershey Derry Township Historical Society Collection.)

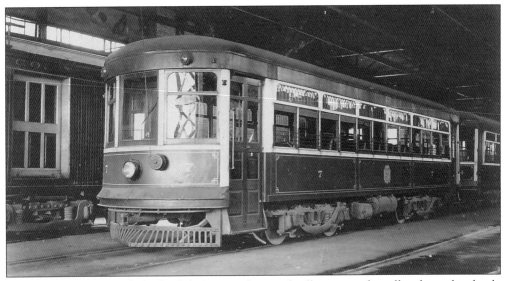

The ornate detail of both the leaded-glass windows and yellow painted scrollwork can be clearly seen on No. 7 in the West Car Barn, date unknown. It is believed that the Hershey Chocolate Company may have aided in the financing of these cars, as it would have been more economical to supply cars to the neighboring Ephrata & Lebanon Traction Company than to construct a separate line to increase access to local dairy farms. (Neil Fasnacht collection.)

Three

THE HUMMELSTOWN LINE

During the spring of 1903, the Hummelstown & Campbellstown Street Railway Company was organized and chartered to construct a trolley line between its namesake towns. The new trolley line would be built with the primary purposes of transporting workers and providing a continuous supply of fresh milk required to keep Milton Hershey's newly built chocolate factory in full production. On October 15, 1904, service was inaugurated and the five-mile trip between Hummelstown and Derry Church was scheduled to take 15 minutes. It was announced in June 1901 that the Harrisburg & Hummelstown Street Railway would lay track from the town of Paxtang to Hummelstown, thereby providing a direct connection between Harrisburg and Derry Church.

By all measures, Milton Hershey's ventures were a success given that the Hummelstown & Campbellstown Street Railway was reported to have carried over 12,400 picnickers to Hershey Park on a single day. By 1907, the street railway owned three cars and had 12 employees. Prosperity continued, and by 1912, additional equipment had been purchased in the form of two new double-truck cars and four secondhand single-truck cars from Baltimore. In May 1912, the Barber Car Company, a trolley manufacturer located in nearby York, provided a newly built internal combustion–powered center-door trolley to the Hummelstown & Campbellstown Street Railway for use on the new extension being constructed between Campbelltown and Lebanon. It appears that the Barber car was not well suited for operation on the Hummelstown & Campbellstown Street Railway, as the car was only in service for a few months before being sent to Ontario in October.

During 1913, the Hummelstown & Campbellstown Street Railway as well as some of the other trolley lines surrounding the town of Hershey were consolidated to form the Hershey Transit Company. In the 1920s, Hershey Transit initiated interline service to provide direct service from Harrisburg and Lancaster to Hershey Park. It was common to see chartered and special-event cars of other trolley lines operate on Hershey Transit rails as they traveled to and from Hershey Park.

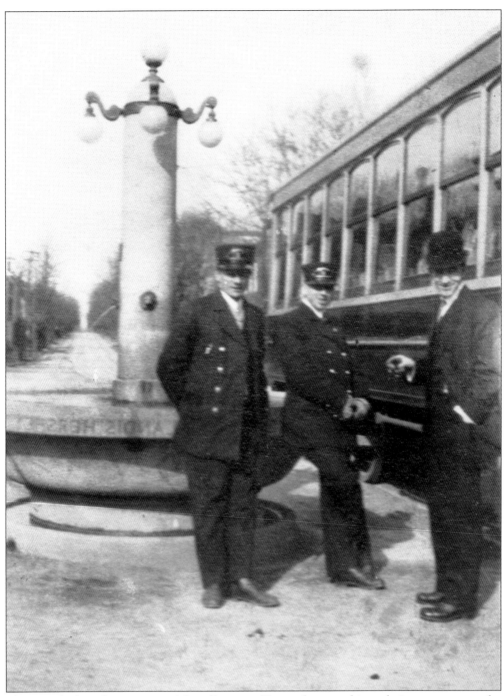

Photographed in the square on Main Street in Hummelstown, this early image captures the Hummelstown & Campbellstown Street Railway motorman and conductor conversing with a local citizen. Prior to the very prominent arch being placed in the square, a horse watering trough, or fountain, stood as the centerpiece. Landis Hershey erected the fountain in memory of his parents. The fountain is still on display in the triangle south of West Main Street on Rosanna Street. (Neil Fasnacht collection.)

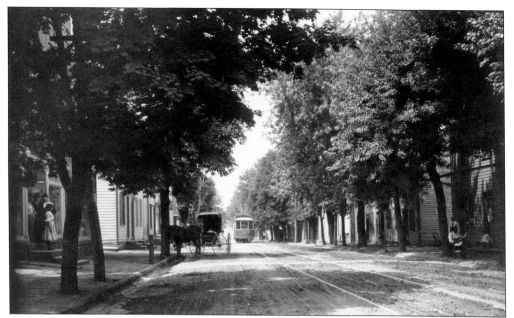

Hummelstown was originally founded as Fredrickstown in 1762 by Frederick and Rosina Hummel, who had purchased the property for 200 pounds sterling. The town was planned and divided into building lots, which were sold mostly to German immigrants. On August 26, 1874, Hummelstown was incorporated as a borough by an act of the state legislature. This is a turn-of-the-20th-century view down Main Street. (Neil Fasnacht collection.)

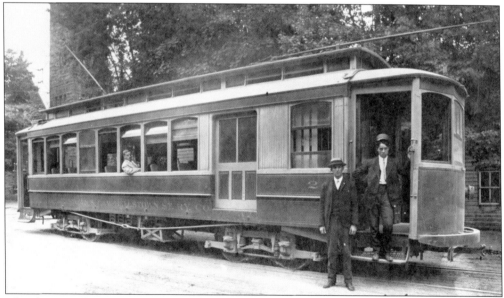

The photographer has captured motorman Harry O'Neal (right) and his conductor posing with No. 2 on West Main Street in Hummelstown. The original Hummelstown & Campbellstown terminal was located at the Philadelphia & Reading Railroad depot on the corner of Second and North Railroad Streets. When Central Pennsylvania Traction Company began service to Hummelstown in 1905, passengers were transferred between the two companies at the corner of Main and Rosanna Streets. (Hershey Derry Township Historical Society Collection.)

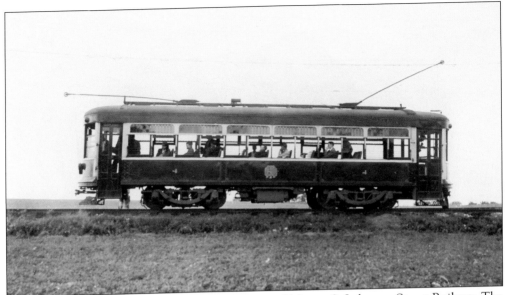

No. 4 came to Hershey Transit from the Lancaster, Ephrata & Lebanon Street Railway. The Lancaster, Ephrata & Lebanon had originally ordered six cars, but two of the cars were canceled. One of these cars, a straight coach, had already been constructed and remained at the Cincinnati Car Company until the Cincinnati Street Railway eventually purchased it in 1918 as No. 1662. (Robert Lawless collection.)

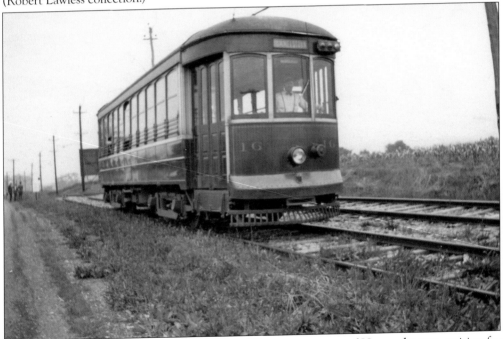

Here, No. 16 holds at the passing siding named Brownstone, east of Hummelstown, waiting for the opposing car to pass. This Brill car was ordered on March 13, 1913, precisely nine months before the official formation of the Hershey Transit Company. The Lebanon & Campbellstown Street Railway, a subsidiary created solely for the purpose of constructing a trolley line between its namesake towns, ordered this car. (Neil Fasnacht collection.)

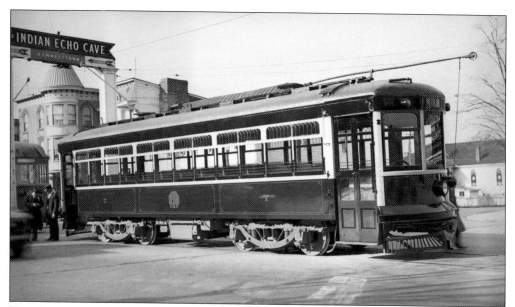

Here, No. 7 (ex–Ephrata & Lebanon No. 21) and Harrisburg Railways No. 70 prepare to depart Hummelstown. Connecting service from Harrisburg was inaugurated on December 15, 1905, but ensuing heavy rains caused washouts along the line. Once track repairs were made, regularly scheduled connecting service to Harrisburg began on December 18. (Milton Hershey School.)

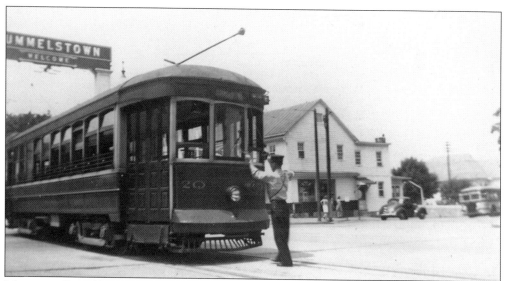

Motorman Russell King is preparing No. 20 for the return trip to Hershey. When a trolley had reached its destination, the motorman needed to change operating ends for the car's return trip. One of the activities to be completed was to change the trolley pole used for collecting electricity from the overhead wire to power the car. (Milton Hershey School.)

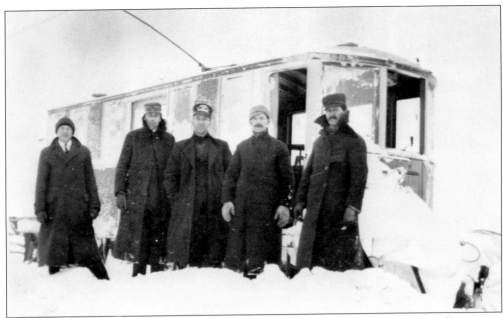

While employing a sweeper to remove snow from the right-of-way can be very efficient, its operation is difficult and labor intensive. This type of car produced a very rough ride for the crew. The motorman, Harry Bistline, is in the center of the photograph; rest of the crew remains to be identified. (Lisa Schirato collection.)

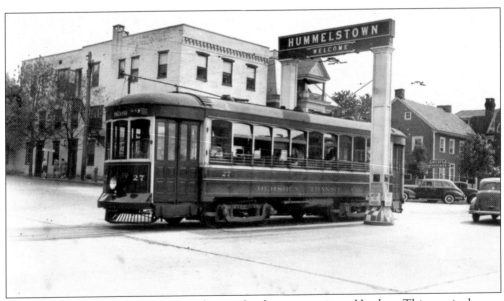

No. 27 is preparing to depart Hummelstown for the return trip to Hershey. This particular car had the distinction of being the last new piece of equipment to be ordered by Hershey Transit. The order for this car, along with car No. 26, was placed on March 3, 1920, with the J.G. Brill Company. These semi-convertible cars, of which Hershey Transit had 12 on the roster, were very versatile and served the community well over the years. Nos. 26 and 27 continued to faithfully fulfill their duties until the end of operations in 1946. (Stan Bowman Jr. collection.)

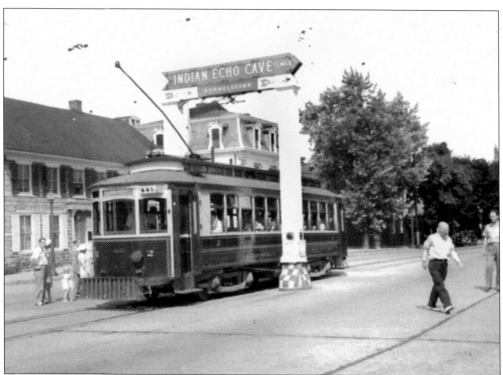

No. 2, a product of the J.G. Brill Company, is captured in the square of Hummelstown under the arch, an icon of the town erected in 1929. The June 24, 1955, edition of the *Hummelstown Sun* reports that the Pennsylvania State Highway Commission had removed the arch. (Andy Maginnis collection.)

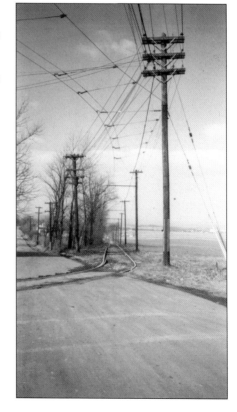

Photographed by Chick Siebert on January 12, 1947, looking north, this is the grade crossing and right-of-way from Hockersville Road on the Hummelstown line. Hershey Transit met up with streetcars from Harrisburg at the Hummelstown terminus in the square on Main Street until February 1937, when buses replaced the trolleys from Harrisburg. (Chick Siebert.)

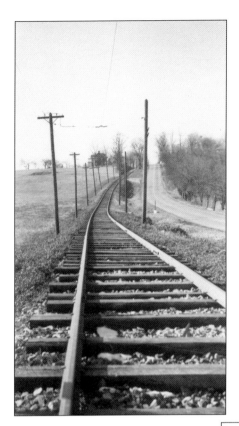

The right-of-way is shown in this view looking west on January 12, 1947, from a point about one quarter mile east of Hummelstown Borough line. Hershey Transit streetcars and its neighboring lines (Conestoga Traction, Reading Street Railway and Harrisburg Railways) ran on a "Pennsylvania Broad Gauge" track (62 1/2 inches), versus the more common standard-gauge track (56 1/2 inches) used by other street railway systems. (Chick Siebert.)

A view looking down Main Street as No. 21 prepares for departure from Hummelstown. The arch directly above the car welcomes all visitors to the town. After its opening to the public in 1929, the sign was altered to direct visitors to Indian Echo Caverns, a popular local tourist attraction. (Hershey Derry Township Historical Society.)

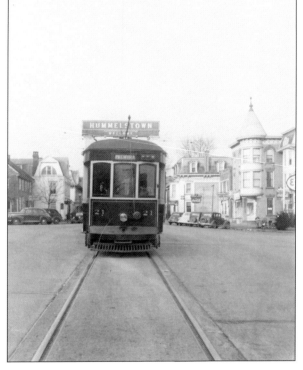

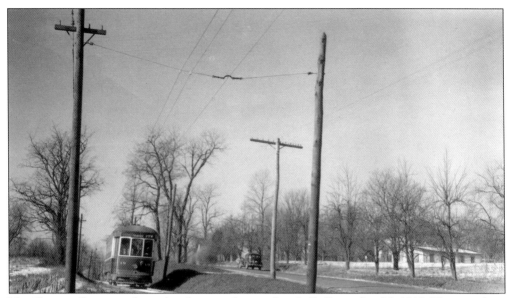

No. 17 is rapidly approaching the photographer on this chilly December 28, 1940. This car, along with No. 16, were the only cars ordered by the Lebanon & Campbellstown Street Railway, a predecessor of the Hershey Transit Company. No. 17 was ordered from the J.G. Brill Company on November 7, 1913, less than one week before the Hershey Transit Company was formed. (Chick Siebert.)

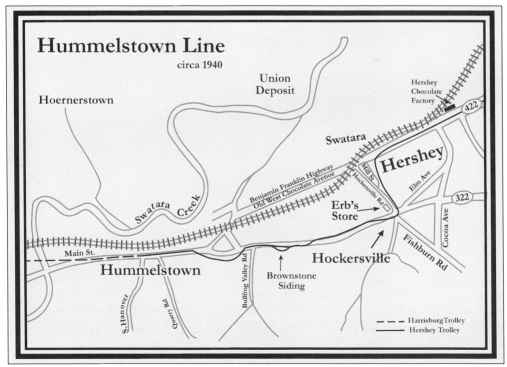

This map shows the Hummelstown Line. (Lauren Fasnacht and Lisa Ginder.)

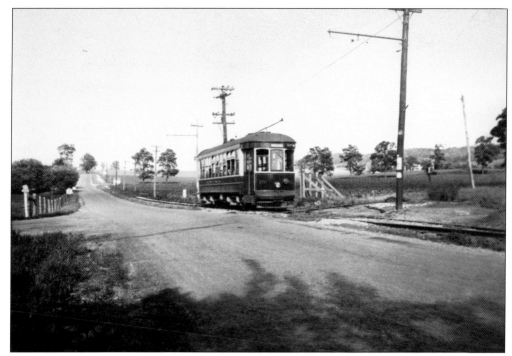

No. 10 is about to pass over the Brownstone & Middletown Railroad crossing east of Hummelstown. The B&M was constructed in 1884–1885 with the primary purpose of conveying the world-famous brownstone from its quarry in Waltonville through Bull Frog Valley to an interchange with the Philadelphia & Reading Railroad. The 2.4-mile railroad ceased operations in 1927. (Neil Fasnacht collection.)

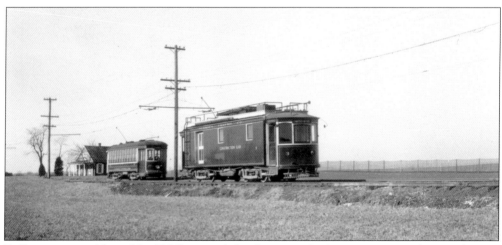

Brill semi-convertible car No. 27 follows out behind No. 3 in the first turnout east of Hummelstown. Both cars were purchased from the J.G. Brill Company. Chick Siebert captured this photograph on December 28, 1940. (Chick Siebert.)

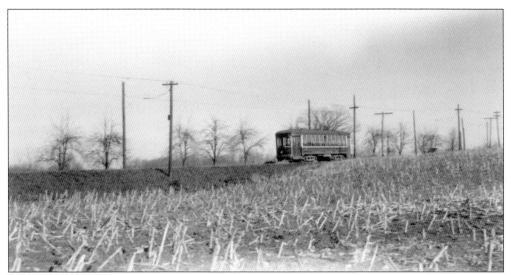

A chill is in the air as No. 27 is making its daily rounds between Hummelstown and Hershey. On this particular day, the day before Christmas Eve 1941, many of the passengers are headed to the Hershey Department Store to complete their purchases in preparation for the holiday. (Chick Siebert.)

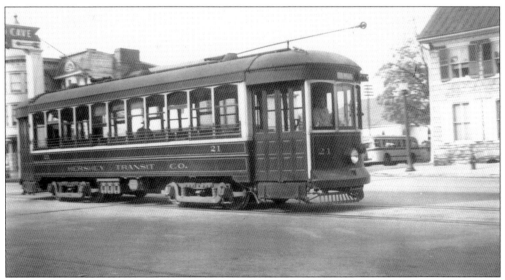

On this frosty Saturday, October 21, 1939, No. 21 waits to depart the Hummelstown square for the 15-minute trip to Hershey. Passengers travelling to Harrisburg were originally transferred at the corner of Main and Rosanna Streets. After Hummelstown & Campbellstown service to the railroad depot was discontinued in 1910, the track along Main Street from Rosanna Street to the square was then leased to Harrisburg Railways. (Chick Siebert.)

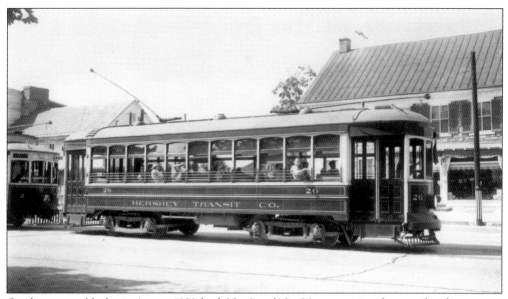

On this seasonable day in August 1939, both No. 2 and No. 26 are awaiting the transfer of passengers from the connecting bus service from Harrisburg. Connecting through trolley service ended on January 10, 1937. Shuttle trolley service between Rutherford and Hummelstown continued until February 6, 1937, while a franchise dispute was being settled. (Chick Siebert.)

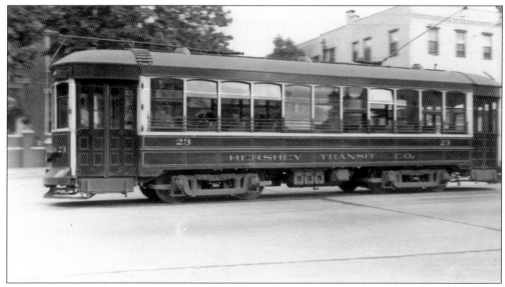

Here, No. 23 is in Hummelstown square waiting to receive passengers connecting from Harrisburg on July 16, 1939. Cars were operated from here to Hershey on an hourly basis. No. 23 was ordered in December 1915 and was virtually identical to the other semi-convertible cars built for Hershey Transit by the J.G. Brill Company. This patented design allowed the car's removable side panels to be stored within the roof during the warmer months of the year. (Chick Siebert.)

Four

THE CAMPBELLTOWN TO LEBANON LINE

The increased need for more fresh milk became evident as chocolate production steadily increased at the factory. A line to Lebanon and the creamery there was soon to be established, and the Lebanon & Campbellstown Street Railway Company was incorporated on August 23, 1911. Harry N. Herr and his crew began the survey of the line. Herr was secured by Milton Hershey to create his new community at Derry Church, Pennsylvania, and would be responsible for the surveying of his streetcar system.

Construction would soon follow. Work began on this particular line in September 1911. Survey for a bridge over the Cornwall Railroad, and the Cornwall & Lebanon Railroad would be secured by Herr and his crew in August 1912.

On January 31, 1913, the first trip to Lebanon was held and car No. 11 was secured for the run. Regularly scheduled service would later be instituted on February 7, 1913. The completed line carried passengers from Campbelltown, thence to Fontana along Route 322, across farm fields and a private right-of-way to Oak Street, near the city of Lebanon, Pennsylvania. It would continue east along Oak Street to a bridge and trestle over the Cornwall Railroad and the Cornwall & Lebanon Railroad to Ninth and Cumberland Streets. The line continued across Cumberland Street toward Willow and down to Eighth Street for freight purposes, but was eventually removed.

Once the Ephrata & Lebanon Traction Company established electric trolley service to Lebanon a few years later, Hershey established a milk station at the village of Lincoln, near Ephrata, in Lancaster County. An agreement between the two trolley companies allowed for freight motors of Hershey Transit to operate over the line. This would continue until March 1, 1929, when the chocolate company added trucks for its milk pickups.

The Lebanon & Campbellstown Street Railway Company and the Hummelstown & Campbellstown Street Railway Company would eventually merge to form the Hershey Transit Company in 1913. At midnight, January 9, 1942, service on the Campbelltown to Lebanon leg of the line was shut down. The line from Hershey to Campbelltown would remain intact, a result of World War II, until the final run of the Hershey Transit on December 21, 1946.

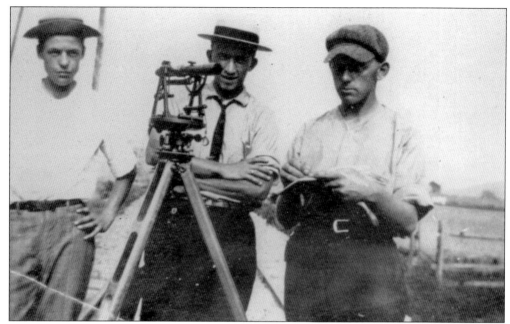

The *Hershey Press* in August 1911 indicated that 17 different firms sent in bids for the construction of the Campbelltown-Lebanon line. The firm of Davis, Barr, and Brightbill won the bid. The survey crew, consisting of George Gerth (middle) and Art Boyer (right), began the arduous task of laying out the right-of-way using the equipment of the day, a surveyor's transit. (Milton Hershey School.)

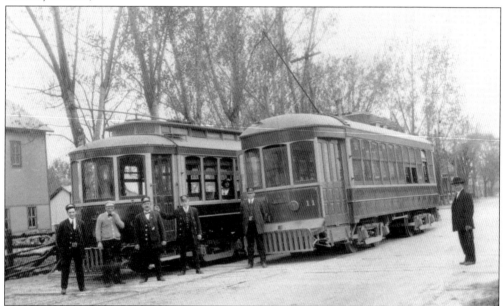

No. 11, a product of the J.G. Brill Company, was built in 1912 for the Hummelstown & Campbellstown Street Railway. Here, it passes what is believed to be No. 2 on its way to Hershey past the Rising Sun restaurant in Campbelltown. The "Sun" is situated on the same spot where Frederick Wolfersberger's Tavern once stood as early as 1794 and remains today a popular eating establishment. (Don Rhoads Jr. collection.)

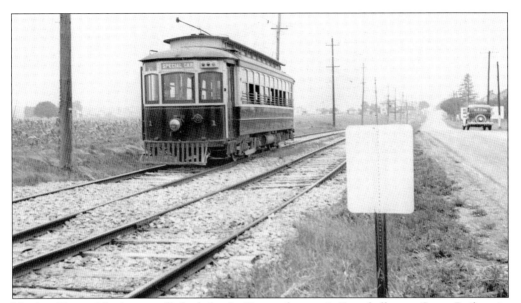

Hershey Transit No. 1, originally built for the Hummelstown & Campbellstown Street Railway in 1903, was photographed by Charles Butler on June 23, 1940, while stopped at the Carmany siding just east of Campbelltown. The route of the trolley followed along the Horseshoe Turnpike, now Route 322, until reaching the next town of Fontana. Originally incorporated as the Downingtown, Ephrata, and Harrisburg Turnpike in 1803, the Horseshoe Turnpike was completed by 1819. (Photograph by Charles Butler; Don Rhoads Jr. collection.)

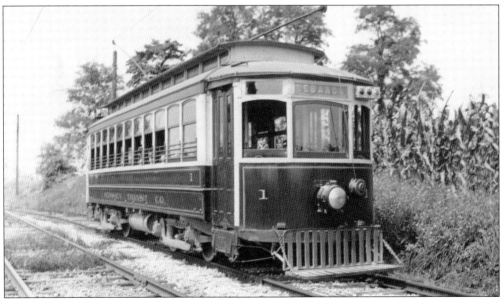

No. 1 was photographed at the Fontana siding on July 20, 1941. The siding, located just north of Route 322, carried riders from here to Lebanon across the countryside. Fontana was located in South Annville Township, Lebanon County, and named by Congressman John W. Killinger in 1872. The fare from Campbelltown to Fontana in 1922 cost 10¢. (Photograph by Charles Butler; Don Rhoads Jr. collection.)

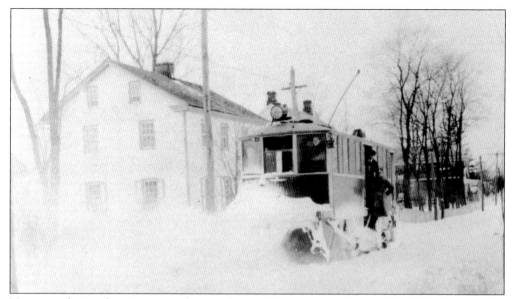

Necessary during the winter months was the use of a snow-sweeping car. No. 15 is shown at the western end of Campbelltown. A product of the J.G. Brill Company, it was built in 1912 for the Hummelstown & Campbellstown Street Railway. Sweepers like this one were outfitted with a cylindrical brush made of bamboo spines, which rotated to remove snow from the rail. (Don Rhoads Jr. collection.)

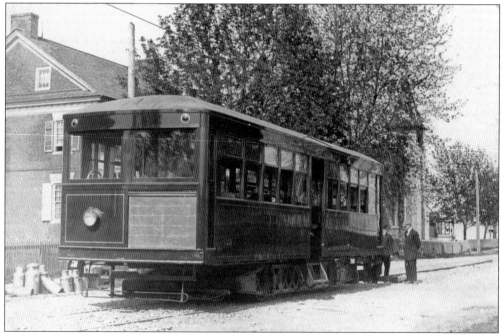

Built by the Barber Car Company of York, Pennsylvania, this single-truck, double-end, center-entrance car arrived on May 8, 1912, and could be used for passenger and freight service. Operating without the use of overhead trolley wire, it had a gasoline engine connected to a generator, which supplied electricity to a motor located on each axle. It began operating on a regular basis May 13, 1912. (Harvey S. Lineaweaver, Don Rhoads Jr. collection.)

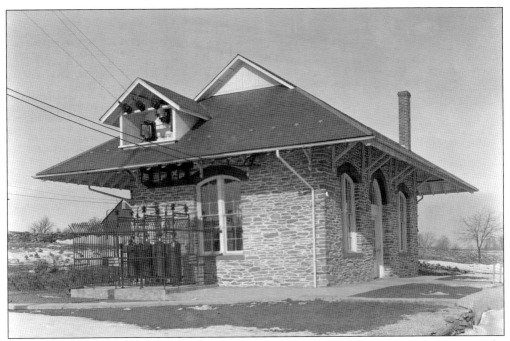

With the extension of the line to Lebanon, a new substation was required to generate power for the overhead wire. The firm of Stohler Brothers of Lebanon was hired to do the masonry work, and James K. Putt of Hershey supervised the construction. The substation was located near the present-day Lebanon Country Club on Oak Street in North Cornwall Township and was fed by high-tension lines carrying 23,000 volts. (Neil Fasnacht collection.)

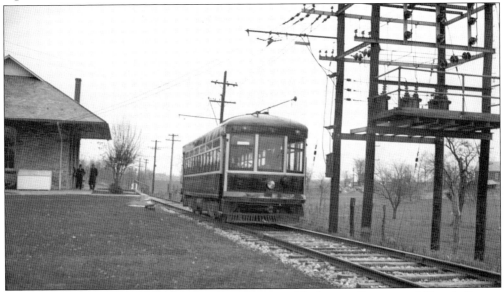

No. 7 stops at the Lebanon substation on its return trip to Hershey via Fontana and Campbelltown. Note the high-tension structure located trackside. The 23,000 volts were supplied to three transformers, connected to a 300-kW, 600-volt, three-phase Westinghouse rotary converter, which was located inside the building. Adjacent to the substation, a five-room residence was built for the operator. (Milton Hershey School.)

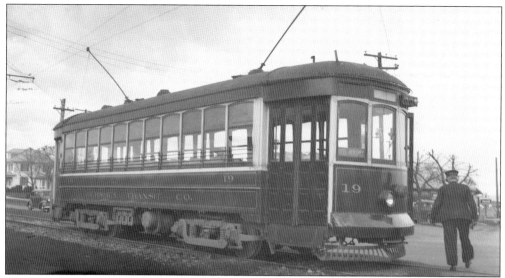

No. 19 appears at the eastern end of Campbelltown in 1940 at a spot still called Leeds Corner by native residents. Harry Leed opened a store at this intersection of State Route 117 and Route 322 in 1924. The store operated under various owners until it closed in 1997. It was the location of the end of the line when the Lebanon division ceased at midnight on January 9, 1942. (Don Rhoads Jr. collection.)

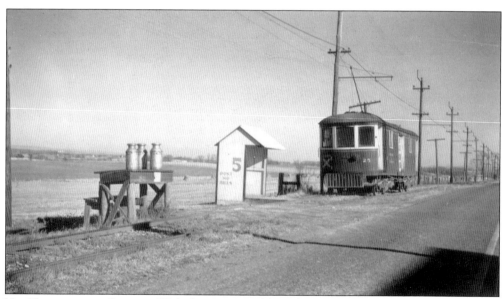

No. 25 appears near Fontana. With the opening of the Lebanon line, and the construction of the Hershey-operated creamery at Tenth Street, express cars were needed. The freight and express car was designed and built by Hershey Transit and was placed in service on Tuesday, March 26, 1918. Farms along the right-of-way constructed platforms to hold milk cans awaiting pickup. Chick Siebert photographed No. 25 in 1940. (Chick Siebert.)

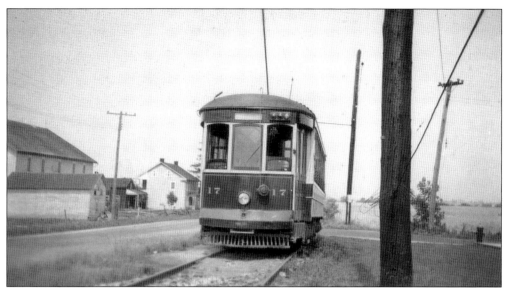

No. 17, a product of the J.G. Brill Company in 1914, appears at Campbelltown in 1946, the last year the trolleys would operate. The farmhouse in the background was built by Samuel Bowman (1814–1879) in 1865, and the barn was constructed a year later. Bowman, a farmer, later operated a store in Campbelltown and was instrumental in establishing Brightbill's United Brethren Church, located along the trolley right-of-way between Campbelltown and Fontana. (Chick Siebert.)

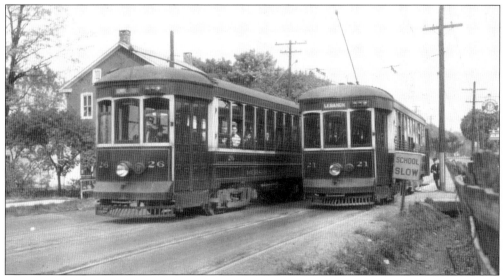

With the extension of the line into Lebanon, a siding was necessary in Campbelltown. It was added in 1913 in front of the Rising Sun. No. 26 and No. 21 were some of the last cars built for Hershey Transit by the J.G. Brill Company and were used until closure of the line in 1946. Chick Siebert captured them at Campbelltown on October 21, 1939, in front of a long, brick home once used to house the owners of a wagon-producing facility. Today, the brick home remains, but the trolleys are long gone. (Chick Siebert.)

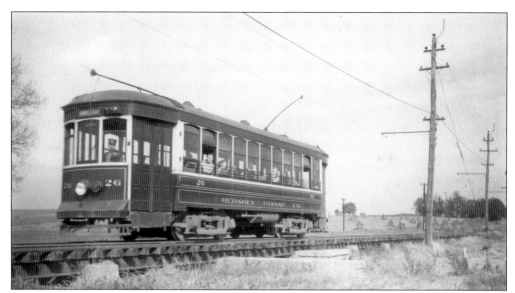

No. 26 arrived in Hershey under its own power on October 21, 1920. Master mechanic William Zimmerman and superintendent John R. Kreider traveled over various lines directly from the Brill plant in Philadelphia. Photographed on October 21, 1939, No. 26 passes over Beck Creek near the Lebanon Country Club on Oak Street. Today, in this vicinity, the trolley right-of-way can still be seen, including the concrete abutments. (Chick Siebert.)

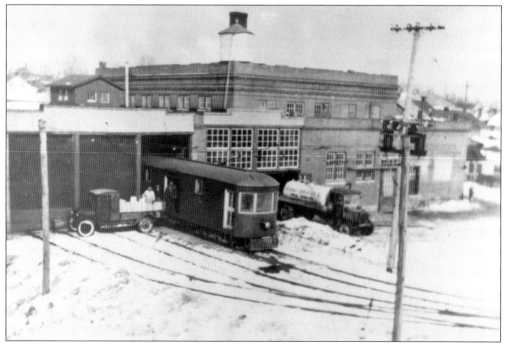

On August 22, 1912, the *Hershey Press* reported that a contract to construct a creamery, condensing plant, carbarn, and residences in Lebanon, Pennsylvania, was awarded to William H. Flick of Lancaster, Pennsylvania. This structure was built to accommodate milk receiving and processing prior to its shipment to the Hershey Chocolate Factory. Freight and express trolleys were used to haul the milk to and from the creamery. (Neil Fasnacht collection.)

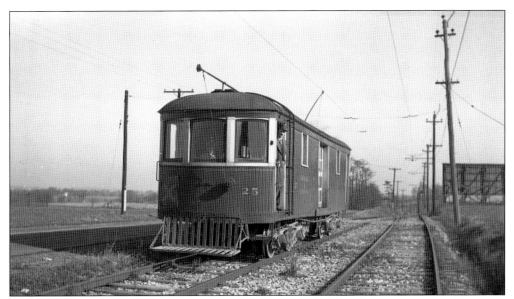

Charles Butler photographed Hershey Transit express motor No. 25 at Carmany siding on November 28, 1941. Butler (who died in 1971) was a native of Clearfield, Clearfield County, Pennsylvania, but resided in Palmyra, Lebanon County, Pennsylvania, most of his adult life. His images captured another place and time, when electric transportation was king. (Photograph by Charles Butler; Don Rhoads Jr. collection.)

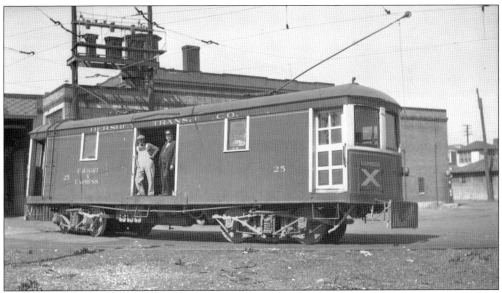

Express No. 25 appears at the Lebanon Creamery on April 25, 1941. Here, the milk from the surrounding dairy farms was gathered, processed, and then shipped to the chocolate factory for final processing into Hershey's chocolate. The transit system would assist with this task, including the use of a special "thermos" on wheels to transport the milk. (Photograph by Charles Butler; Don Rhoads Jr. collection.)

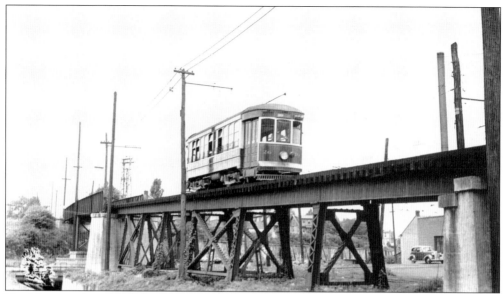

No. 26 arrives from Hershey via Campbelltown and Fontana on the trestle specially constructed to carry the trolley cars over the Cornwall Railroad and the Cornwall & Lebanon Railroad (later the Pennsylvania Railroad) tracks at Lebanon. The line would swing sharply to the left after descending toward Ninth Street to access the creamery. Today, one of the concrete abutments that supported the steel structure remains. (Stan Bowman Jr. collection.)

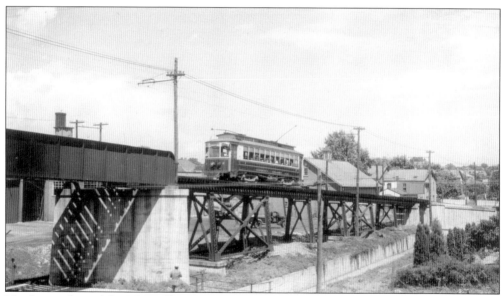

No. 2, a product of the J.G. Brill Company purchased by the Hummelstown & Campbellstown Street Railway, leaves Lebanon and ascends the trestle toward Oak Street. According to the *Hershey Press*, the survey for the location of the trestle was made in August 1912. Chick Siebert captured this scene in 1939. (Chick Siebert.)

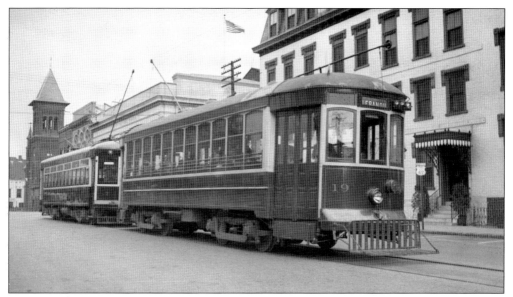

On November 22, 1936, No. 19 and No. 7 are being readied for the return trip to Hershey. The terminus of Hershey Transit originally carried the cars across Ninth and Cumberland Streets to Willow Street, east on Willow, terminating at North Eighth Street. It would later be cut back to a terminus at Ninth and Cumberland Streets. The Eagle Hotel, in the right background, was owned by Josiah Funck and was later renamed the Hotel Weimer. It remained a part of Lebanon's scene until being torn down in 1963 for a public parking lot. (Milton Hershey School.)

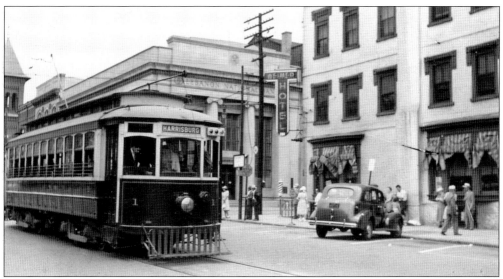

No. 1 appears on the south side of Ninth and Cumberland Streets. The car's roll sign indicates Harrisburg for the return trip, but the Hershey Transit connected with the Harrisburg Railways cars at Hummelstown. The Lebanon National Bank across Cumberland Street was organized as the Lebanon Bank on May 21, 1831. It moved to the Ninth Street location in 1884, and the structure seen in the photograph was built in 1926. Today, the building remains, but the bank no longer exists. (Milton Hershey School.)

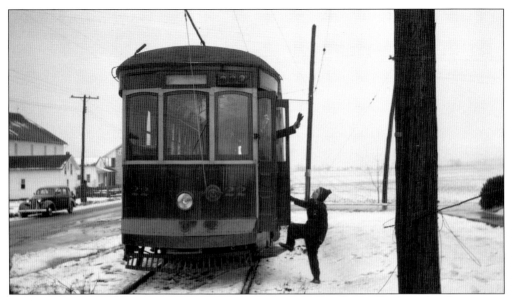

Photographer Charles Butler captured No. 22 at Campbelltown on the last day of trolley service, December 21, 1946. Motorman Owen Hughes (1889–1953) waves goodbye as young Barbara Bordlemay waits her turn to climb aboard. Hughes began his career with the system in 1911. In 1917, he entered World War I and served until 1919, when he returned and worked for Hershey Transit until 1946. In 1919, he married Alma Miller, daughter of Campbelltown's saddler, George Miller. (Photograph by Charles Butler; Don Rhoads Jr. collection.)

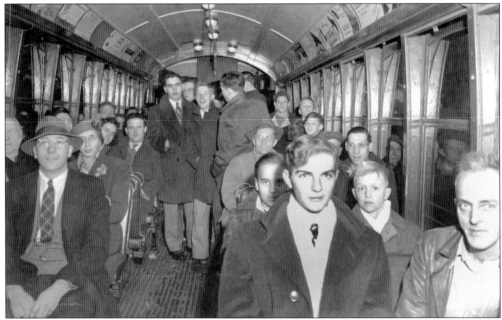

Residents of Campbelltown and students from the Hershey Industrial School gathered for the last run of Hershey Transit just before midnight on December 21, 1946. John N. Cassel, an employee of Hershey Transit since 1919, served as conductor and motorman. According to the *Patriot*, a number of teenage boys blew the whistle so many times the air pressure dropped, causing the emergency brakes to apply. (Don Rhoads Jr. collection.)

Five

THE BARNS

Over the course of Hershey Transit operations, three carbarns were erected to house the streetcars that provided a mode of transportation for the community of Derry Township. The first of three was designed by well-known architect C. Emlen Urban and stood on the north side of East Chocolate Avenue, adjacent to the offices of the Hershey Chocolate Company. Constructed with limestone, a very popular building material in the area at that time, the carbarn had one large bay that opened at the west end of the structure.

By 1910, Milton Hershey's streetcars had outgrown their first home and a new carbarn, also built from limestone, was erected across the street from the chocolate factory on the south side of Chocolate Avenue. This new barn was 50 feet by 185 feet, and had three bays that opened on the north side with tracks that ran the full length of the building and enough space for 12 cars.

Once again, the trolleys outgrew their home, and in 1916, work began on the West Car Barn, located at the far west end of town and on the north side of Chocolate Avenue. *Electric Traction* stated in January 1917, "The shop will have the most modern and complete equipment for the proper care and repair of cars." The West Car Barn, still standing today, was originally 95 feet by 275 feet, of "modern design," and made with reinforced concrete and brick, making it "absolutely fireproof." This barn had five bays, all with track, three of which were storage track, and two bays with pits that ran the full length of the building. The north side of the barn contained the office, men's locker room with showers, blacksmith shop, machine shop, and storage room. The incorporation of natural light throughout this building is evident in the placement and number of windows.

Today, the West Car Barn is owned by the Hershey Company, never changing ownership since its conception during Milton S. Hershey's lifetime. Friends of the Hershey Trolley currently use space in this barn for shop work restoration and storage of cars No. 3 and No. 7, as well as the original Hershey Park Miniature Railway.

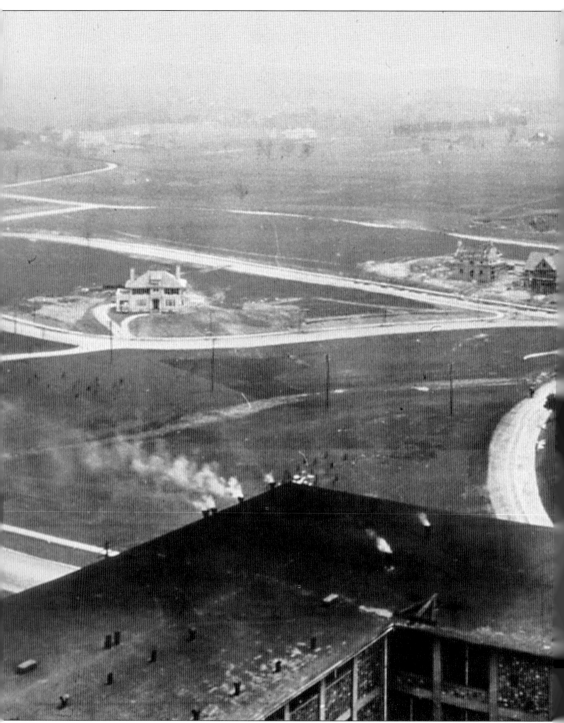

Looking south across Chocolate Avenue from the roof of the young chocolate factory complex in 1914, one can see the second carbarn, designed by C. Emlen Urban, with its prominent three bays on the right of the photograph. On the left side of the carbarn is an addition that was built in December 1914. This addition contained an office, storage room, and machine shop. Java

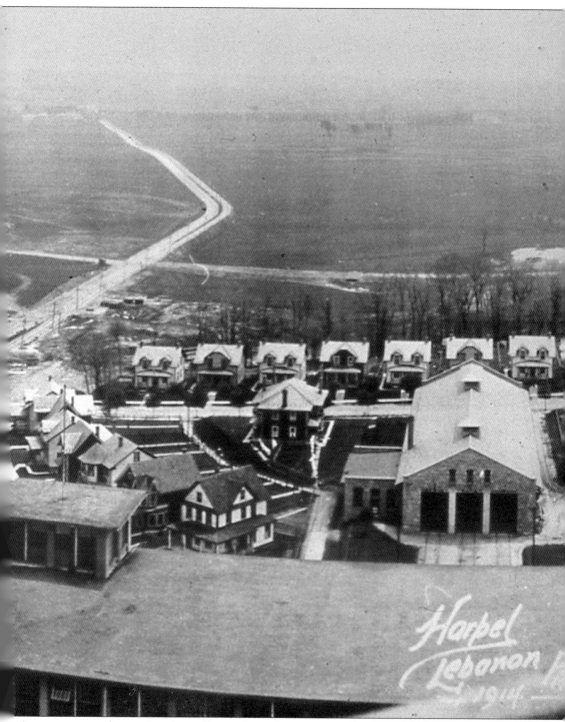

Avenue runs south carrying the trolley tracks and connects to the second carbarn. Homestead Road to the left of Java carries other modes of transportation in and out of the town of Hershey. Large homes to the left are being built for Hershey Chocolate Company management. (Harpel, Hershey Derry Township Historical Society Collection.)

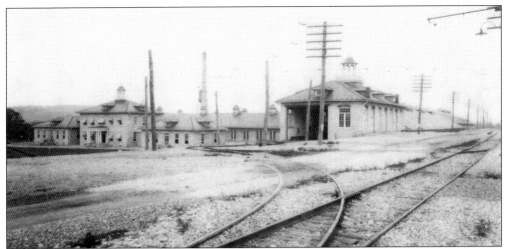

Looking east on Chocolate Avenue, Derry Church, Pennsylvania, about 1904, the first car barn was designed by architect C. Emlen Urban and built by the engineering firm of Francis Bros. & Jellett, Inc., for the Hummelstown and Campbellstown Street Railway Company. In 1909, the street railway out grew the first barn and this building was transformed into the Hershey Café, which served the employees of the Hershey Chocolate Company until 1911, when the café was opened to the public. (Neil Fasnacht collection.)

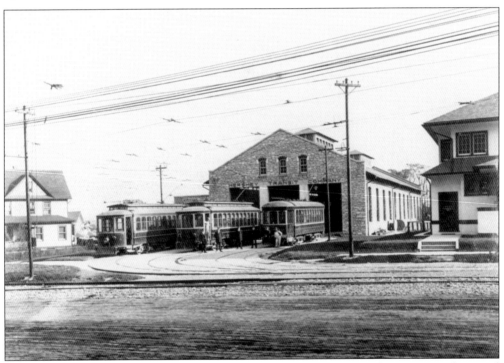

The second of three carbarns, built in 1909, was made of concrete and limestone, and situated on the south side of Chocolate Avenue, across from the chocolate factory, where Java Avenue intersected with Chocolate. With three bays, at 180 feet by 56 feet, this new barn had enough space for 12 streetcars. In 1916, once the fleet outgrew this barn, the building was re-adapted into a garage and eventually apartments. (Neil Fasnacht collection.)

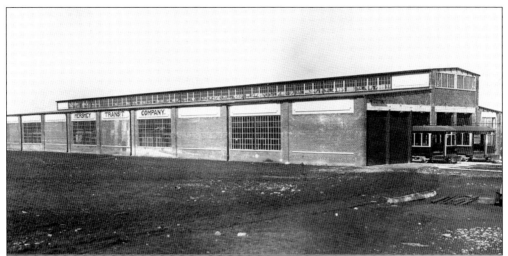

With Robert Deichler overseeing the construction, the West Car Barn, made with reinforced concrete and brick, was the largest and final car barn built for the Hershey Transit Company in 1916. The January 1917 edition of *Electric Traction* states, "The shop will have the most modern and complete equipment for the proper care and repair of cars." The barn was capable of housing up to 40 cars. This is one of several builders' photographs. (Neil Fasnacht collection.)

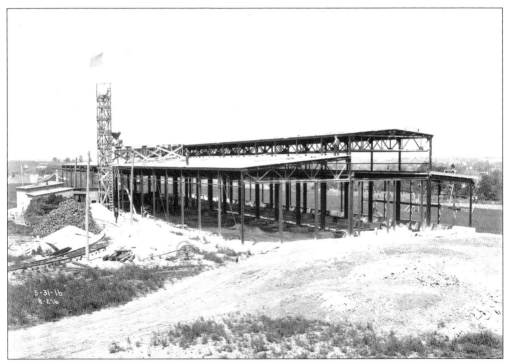

The West Car Barn is located on the northwest end of town between Chocolate Avenue and the railroad tracks. The two center tracks were equipped with a traveling crane and the pits arranged so that heating pipes were free of obstruction and the workmen were not in danger of getting burned. The pit lighting system was recessed into the sidewalls, providing direct and upward lighting onto the bottom of the cars. (Neil Fasnacht collection.)

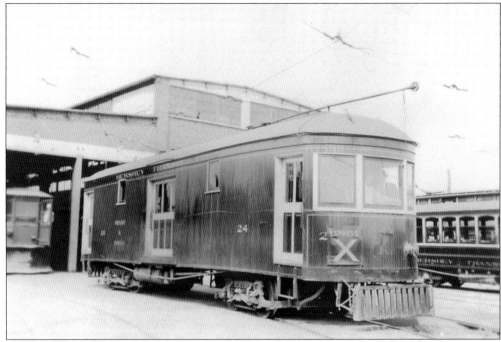

Freight express No. 24, constructed in 1915 by the Hershey Transit Company shop forces, awaits departure from the yard at the West Car Barn on August 20, 1939. The overall car length was 40 feet, with an arch-style roof. (Andy Maginnis collection.)

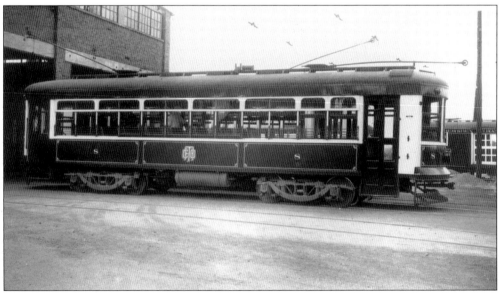

Photographed by Chick Siebert at the West Car Barn on August 13, 1938, No. 8, formerly No. 30 on the Lancaster, Ephrata & Lebanon Street Railway, awaits departure. Built originally as a combination car by the Cincinnati Car Company in 1914, No. 8 was converted to straight passenger in Hershey. Like its sister cars, No. 7 and No. 4, Hershey No. 8 has the distinctive scroll-designed "HTC" painted in yellow on each side of the car. (Chick Siebert.)

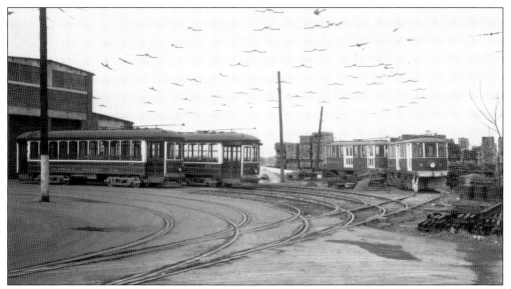

The car yard at the east end of the West Car Barn, three weeks after the last ride, was photographed by Chick Siebert on January 12, 1947. Notice the intricate construction of the overhead trolley wire and the special trackwork required for the movement of cars around the yard and into the five tracks of the carbarn. (Chick Siebert.)

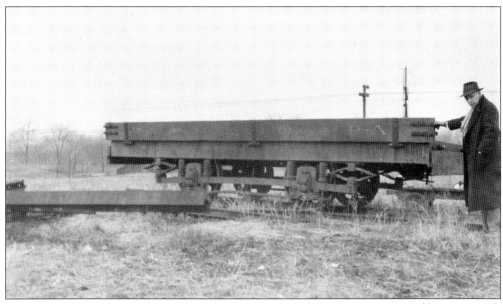

Photographs of Hershey Transit work equipment are relatively uncommon. Pictured here on March 17, 1940, is No. 9-A, a flatcar equipped with a Brill 21-E truck. The records are not clear, but there are indications that this car was rebuilt by Hershey Transit from No. 8, a single-truck car capable of carrying 28 people, purchased secondhand from Baltimore in 1910. (Neil Facnacht collection.)

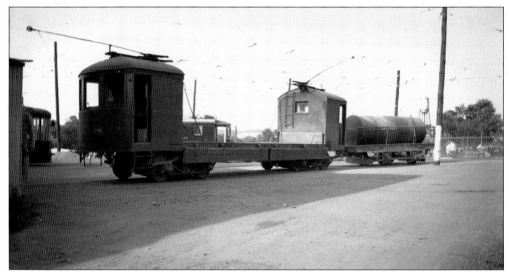

No. 28 was converted from a box motor by the Hershey Traction Company in the early 1930s for the purpose of hauling brick, stone, and other heavy materials. The history of this car is unknown, but records indicate that it was a Brill product built as a box motor in 1915 and may have come to Hershey by way of the Lancaster, Ephrata & Lebanon Street Railway, where it had sat unused from the time it was purchased secondhand in 1922. (Chick Siebert.)

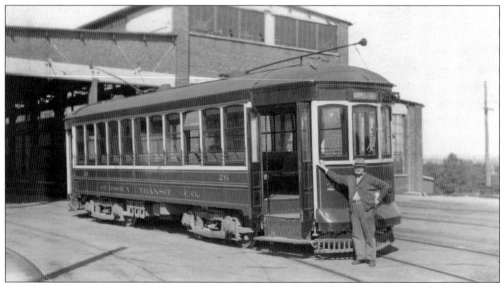

Another semi-convertible car, No. 26, is pictured at the West Car Barn in 1941. The term *semi-convertible* refers to the type of window system installed on the car. The windows were designed to be easily raised and concealed in pockets built into the roof for storage during the warmer months of the year. (Chick Siebert.)

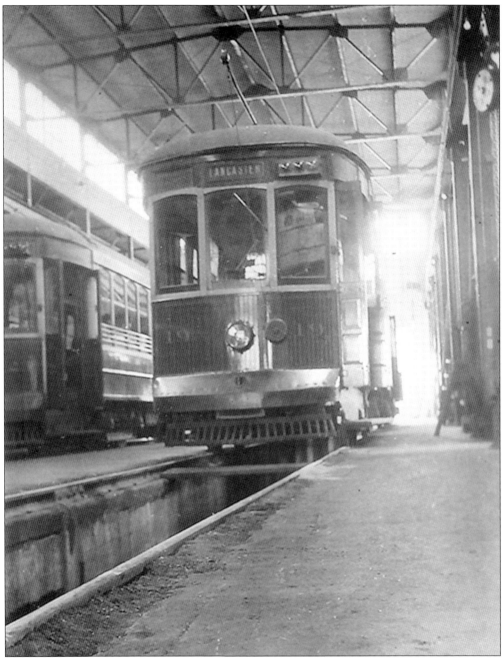

No. 19 was part of a two-car order in October 1914 that was later expanded to four after the initial order was placed. One of many Brill semi-convertible, wooden arch roof–style cars, No. 19 ran until the end in 1946. This image captures the car on the northernmost track at the West Car Barn on an unknown date. (Neil Fasnacht collection.)

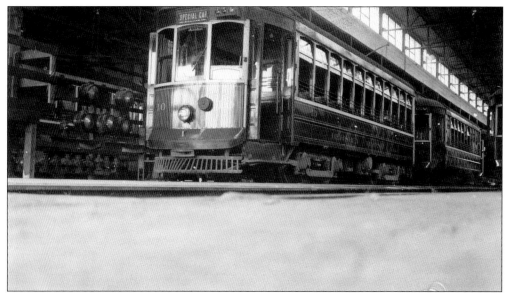

No. 10 was ordered in June 1912 from the J.G. Brill Company. When this car was completed at the factory, chances are that it traveled to Hershey under its own power in late 1912. The car is shown at the West Car Barn during July 1941. It would continue to dutifully serve Hershey Transit for another four years before being retired. (Neil Fasnacht collection.)

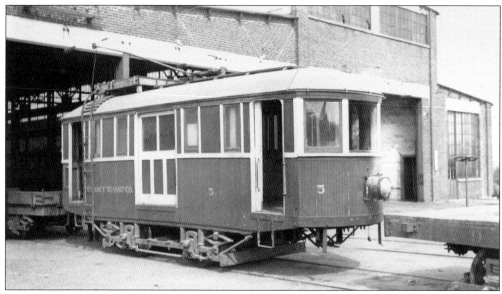

Some early photographs of this car show it configured as a combine. Seen here is No. 5, a work car constructed by the shop by rebuilding a closed passenger car purchased from United Railway of Baltimore in 1908. Hershey Transit was fortunate to have a highly skilled and able shop force. The car had been equipped for use as a snowplow but was determined to be unsuitable for this activity. The car was retired from service in 1941. (Neil Fasnacht collection.)

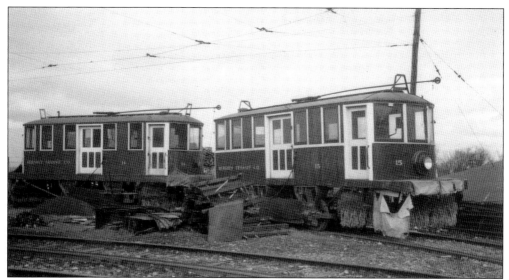

Pictured here on January 12, 1947, after the Hershey Transit system ceased operations, are No. 14 and No. 15 at the West Car Barn. These sweepers were ready to assist in keeping the line clear when the snow started to fall. No. 14 was purchased from neighboring Harrisburg Railways in 1939, and No. 15 was from a stock order; it was constructed by the J.G. Brill Company and purchased by Hershey Transit Company in 1912. (Chick Siebert.)

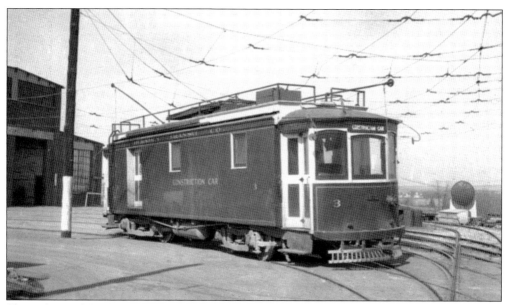

Shown here is No. 3, a unique car since it was the only piece of equipment that would be used in service for the entire existence of the Hershey Transit Company (along with its predecessor, the Hummelstown & Campbellstown). The car was delivered to Hummelstown & Campbellstown as a combine car and, at some point, was converted to a straight coach. In 1928, the Hershey Transit Company found itself in need of additional maintenance equipment and converted No. 3 again, this time as construction car. (Stan Bowman Jr. collection.)

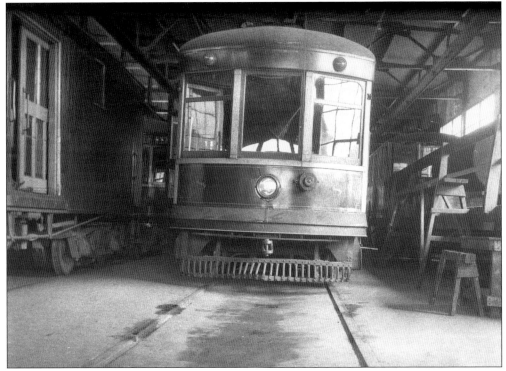

No. 8 is captured in the car barn at rest between revenue service runs. Popular with patrons, the cars were used daily mostly for runs to Palmyra and on the Hotel Line and would see service until the end of operations in December 1946. The car, along with both of its sisters, would escape the scrapper's torch and continue to provide service to people for decades to come, although not carrying passengers to their destinations. (Lisa Schirato collection.)

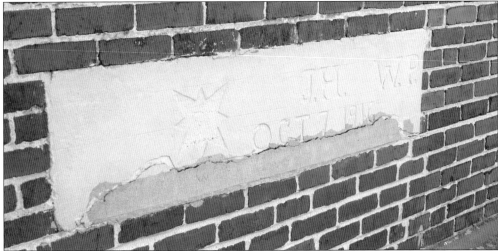

Little is known about this date stone for October 7, 1916, located on the northwest corner of the West Car Barn, facing due north. The October 5, 1916, edition of the *Hershey Press* states in a column titled Facts About Hershey, "Hershey Transit Company, connections east and west, 36 miles of track; southern extension to Lancaster county new. Trolleys every half hour." The photograph was taken in February 2011. (Lisa Schirato.)

Six

MILTON HERSHEY SCHOOL AND THE TROLLEYS

When Milton and Catherine Hershey created the Hershey Industrial School in 1909, they felt strongly that it be both a home and a school. The Hersheys gave boys, ages four through eight, who had lost a father, "real homes, real comforts, education, and training, so they would be useful and happy citizens," as Milton Hershey states in a 1924 *Liberty Magazine* article. Hershey dreamed of helping 100 boys and saw the school grow to 1,000 before he died in 1945. What started with four boys in Milton Hershey's birthplace, The Homestead, has grown to nearly 1,900 boys and girls.

As the school expanded, The Homestead became the administrative office. A trolley line that ran from Campbelltown to Hershey along Horseshoe Pike passed in front of The Homestead and allowed trolleys to deliver goods to the school. Hershey took advantage of the transit system when arranging for the first school dentist by accepting the dentist's offer of free dental care for the students if the school would provide his dental supplies and pay his trolley fare.

In the early days of the school, Hershey housed the students in private homes, first in Kinderhaus, located east of The Homestead. The boys were familiar with seeing the trolleys travel past their homes. One alumnus said he enjoyed sitting on the Kinderhaus porch as a fourth-grade student in the late 1930s observing passing cars, mounted state police, and the trolleys. On special occasions, the boys boarded the trolley right across the street from Kinderhaus to go to Hersheypark. Another graduate said he treasures the memory of being on the trolley when Milton Hershey got on at The Homestead, held him on his lap, talked with him, and when getting off the trolley said, "Have a good day, son."

In 1929, students in grades six through 12 began to live on dairy farms and ride the trolleys into town. When the Junior-Senior High School on Pat's Hill opened in 1934, the students who lived in homes along the line rode the trolley to the school.

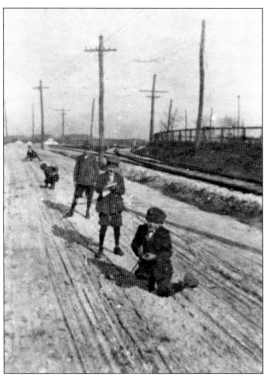

Harold Cool, the first Hershey Industrial School teacher, took his 20 students on hikes and completed hands-on activities, learning how to measure along the trolley line. Cool rode the trolley to school in the morning and sometimes even had the opportunity to operate it—when the motorman was in a good mood.

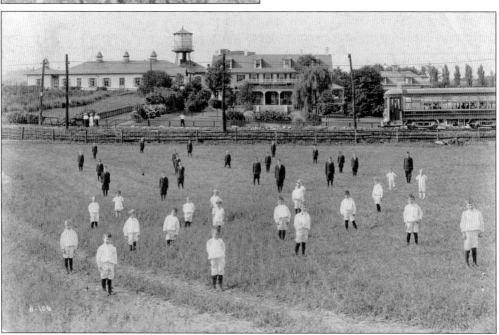

In its first five years, the school grew to an enrollment of 40 boys. In this 1914 photograph, students pose along Horseshoe Pike across from The Homestead. The conductor and passengers of No. 11, visible on the right, watched the photo shoot from the train. Truck patch gardens to the left of The Homestead stretched along Horseshoe Pike and supplied the school with vegetables throughout the year.

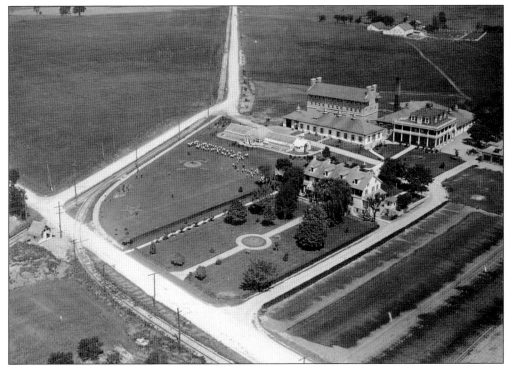

By 1923, the growing school campus included a new building, Ivanhoe; the former experimental chocolate factory called "The Main;" the former dairy barn turned into classrooms; and a greenhouse. This aerial photograph shows the H.I.S. boys lined up to form the word "Hershey." Even though the campus was a short distance from town, the trolley line connected the school to Hershey and beyond.

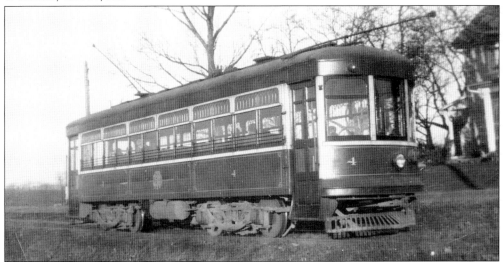

Milton Hershey believed that environment rather than heredity determined what a boy became and that the healthiest environment was on a farm. In 1929, the first farm homes opened for boys in grades 6–12. The trolleys enabled students in homes along the route to ride instead of walk into town. Trolley No. 4 is pictured in front of farm home No. 31, Men-O, located between Hershey and Campbelltown on the Horseshoe Pike.

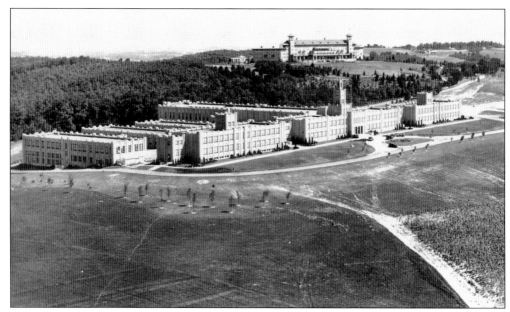

Milton Hershey envisioned a school building on Pat's Hill long before one was constructed, and the dream came true when the Junior-Senior High School was dedicated on November 15, 1934. Transporting construction materials was no problem because trolley tracks already existed on the hill. The structure contained an impressive marble entry, an auditorium that used local lumber, vocational shops, a swimming pool, and design elements consistent with its architectural details.

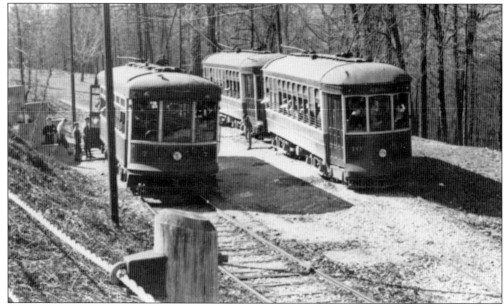

The student-produced publication, the *School Industrialist*, reported a unique feature of the new school: "To do away with precariousness of crossing the road, a subway is being built . . . for the use of those students who utilize the streetcars of the Hershey Transit Company." Students entered the tunnel at the trolley and came out in the school building. In this photograph, students are exiting the tunnel and boarding the trolleys.

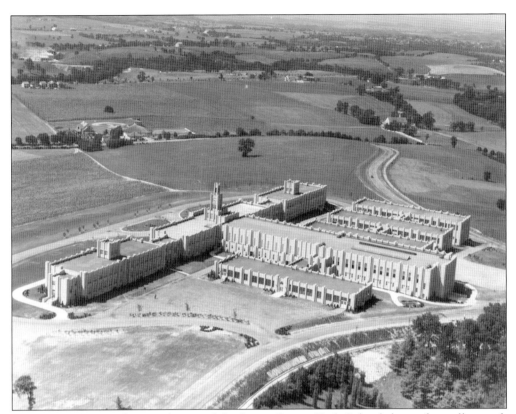

Looking southwest, this aerial view of the Junior-Senior High School shows the trolley track adjacent to the road that wound around the rear of the building, where the tunnel was located, and then down Pat's Hill.

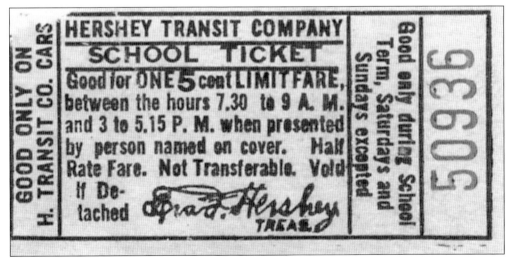

Students were issued trolley tickets to be used to and from school; other trips had to be paid from their allowances. Boys who lived in farm homes on the east side of Hershey walked more than a mile farther east to Palmdale and then took the trolley west into Hershey. Milton Hershey's cousin Ezra Hershey, treasurer of the Hershey Chocolate Company, signed this school transit ticket.

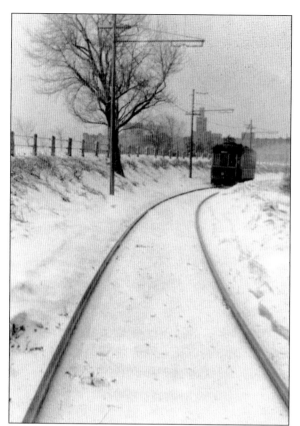

During the gas shortages of World War II, some students who lived in farm homes not on the trolley route walked into town and rode the trolley to and from the Junior-Senior High School, which is visible behind the trolley. Students in the baking vocational program got off the trolley at the Hershey Arena, where the bakeshop was housed.

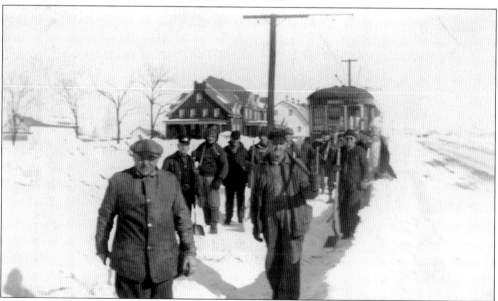

The school's alumni have said that traveling by trolley was better than riding the bus and possibly more dependable in the winter. Here, a team of men clears the track at farm home No. 61, Rolling Green, along Horseshoe Pike. In addition, the transit system not only helped the school, it benefited families of students who did not own a car.

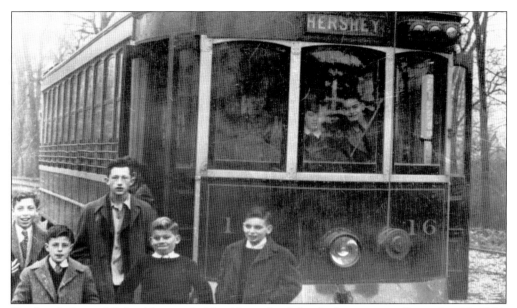

Hershey Industrial School boys rode No. 16 to school for the last time on December 20, 1946. Alumnus Rodger Fredrick, class of 1950, remembers that the operator, Dan Geib, had candy treats for them and took this photograph. The trolleys fascinated Fredrick, and the operators allowed him to operate them on occasion. A lifelong enthusiast, he donated his collection of trolley photographs and collectables to Milton Hershey School.

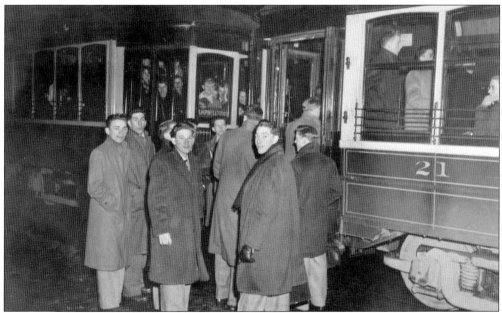

H.I.S. students' last ride is described in the student-produced *School Industrialist:* "A capacity crowd of nostalgic passengers enjoyed the final run. Among them were a number of Homeboys returning from the senior class Christmas Dance. The Hershey streetcars have played a memorable part in the life of H.I.S. boys, and it is with fond memories that we see them depart . . . many a year will pass before they are forgotten."

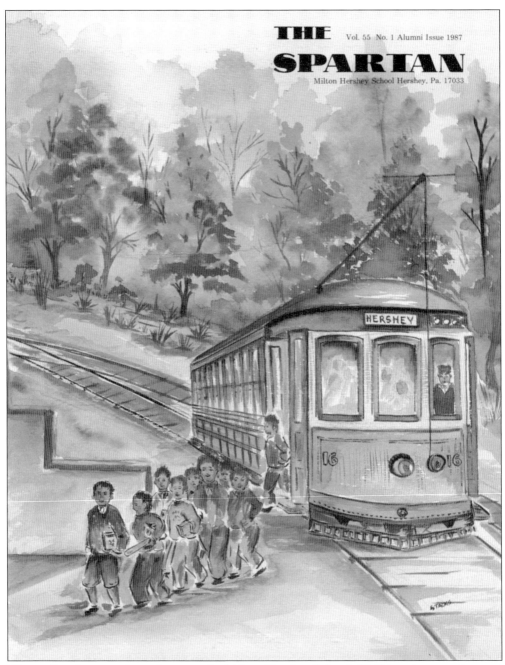

THE SPARTAN

Vol. 55 No. 1 Alumni Issue 1987

Milton Hershey School Hershey, Pa. 17033

The trolleys have not been forgotten by Milton Hershey School. Well-loved art teacher and popular folk artist Clyde Stacks re-created the scene of students going from the trolley into the Junior-Senior High School as a watercolor with gold and brown fall foliage. A print of the painting served as the cover for the *Spartan*, a student-produced publication, in 1987. The issue also includes trolley trivia, asking if readers remember "cow-catchers, sanding the track, losing power while climbing Pat's Hill, and putting your ear to the track to hear if a trolley was coming." Alumni enjoy sharing their treasured memories of the trolleys, and current Milton Hershey School students find the stories fascinating.

Seven

THE ELIZABETHTOWN LINE

On November 11, 1915, the front page of the *Hershey Press* announced that the long-awaited trolley line to Elizabethtown would open in a few days. The new line was to diverge from the Lebanon line at the Hershey Homestead, so that the distance from there to Elizabethtown was 9.75 miles. The fare was 20¢ each way, and the scheduled time for running hourly service in each direction was 30 minutes. This new line made it possible to connect with the trolley line to Lancaster—welcome news for many of Milton Hershey's colleagues who came from the Lancaster area to join his chocolate industry in Hershey. The line was designed to travel through dairy farmland to provide dependable milk delivery to the chocolate factory as well as provide transportation for factory workers living in farms throughout the valley.

By December 1, 1915, the system was comprised of 36 miles of track, making it possible to go by trolley to Lancaster and Philadelphia. Through an arrangement with neighboring Conestoga Traction Company, cars could be run from Hershey to Lancaster and back, without changing to other cars, for special and private parties to Hershey Park located at the north end of Hershey.

Students from the country school known as Vian were now able to travel to the new school in Hershey on the Elizabethtown line, and Vian was closed. Following the abandonment of the Elizabethtown line, Hershey Transit continued to provide trolley service to and from Vian for the benefit of the students until February 24, 1943, and the remainder of track between Homestead and Vian was abandoned immediately. The round-trip fare cost the students 5¢ one way. The trolley system would eventually affect other country schools in Derry Township.

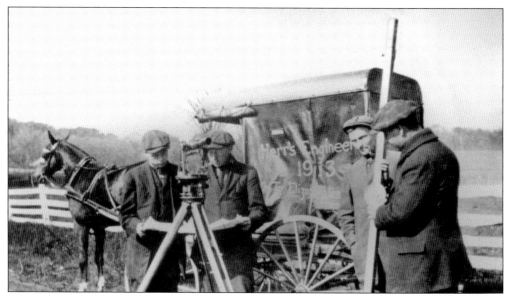

Preliminary surveying by Herr's Engineers for the Elizabethtown line began in 1913. Pictured from left to right are Chas Miller, Artman Boyer, Mr. Smith, and John Black. The November 11, 1915, edition of the *Hershey Press* reports, "The Hershey trolley line to Elizabethtown will be open in a few days. . . . The fare from Hershey to Elizabethtown will be 20 cents each way, or 17 and a fraction cents when tickets are used." (Hershey Derry Township Historical Society Collection.)

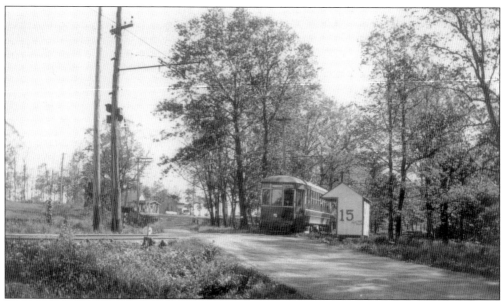

Here is No. 22 passing over a grade crossing near Elizabethtown. The June 1916 edition of *Brill* magazine states, "The present rolling stock, including the new cars, is made up of fourteen double-truck Semi-Convertible Brill cars, two single-truck cars, four milk cars, and snow-fighting apparatus consisting of a sweeper and a plow." (Dick Steinmetz, Chick Siebert collection.)

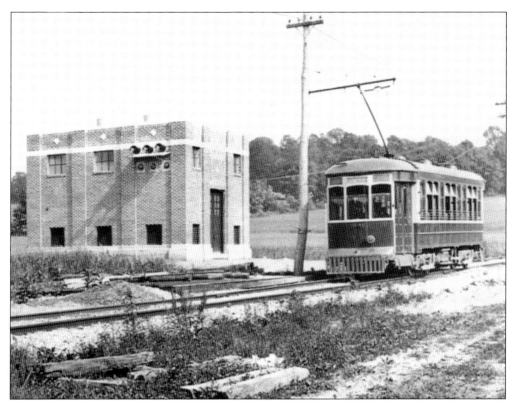

One of the substations constructed to provide power to the overhead trolley wire, this facility was located in Beverly and remains standing to this day, although it is being used for a different purpose. An early Brill car passes the substation on its way to Elizabethtown. (Neil Fasnacht collection.)

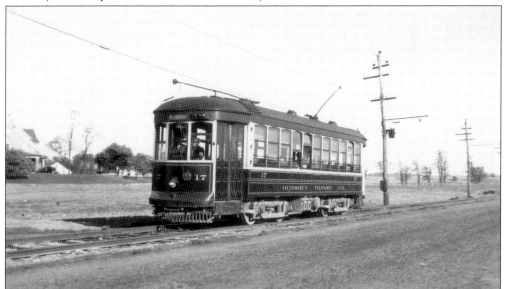

On May 6, 1938, No. 17 passes in front of the old Hershey Industrial School, currently known as The Homestead, birthplace of Milton S. Hershey, near the Lebanon and Elizabethtown junction. (Chick Siebert.)

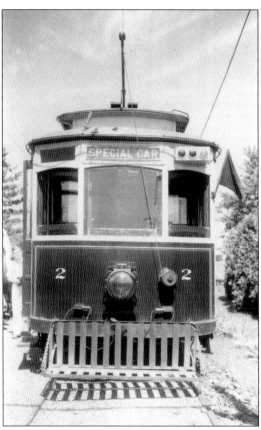

No. 2 sits at the end of the Elizabethtown line during the National Railway Historical Society fan trip on August 13, 1939. (Chick Siebert.)

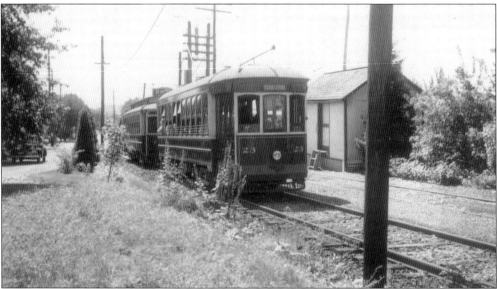

Captured for history are No. 23 and No. 2 at the terminus in Elizabethtown. No 23 is operating as the regularly scheduled car to Hershey, while No 2 is operating as an extra movement while performing the honorable duty of transporting trolley fans during the National Railway Historical Society fan trip. (Chick Siebert.)

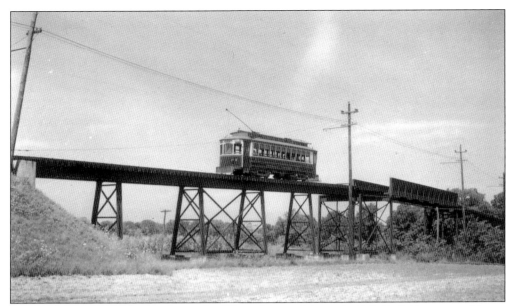

No. 2 is pictured on the Beverly trestle. When delivered from the J.G. Brill Company, this car was configured as a combination car, capable of carrying both passengers and freight. When the amount of freight required the purchase of additional equipment dedicated to hauling freight and milk, No. 2 and identical car No. 3 were then converted to straight passenger cars. Doing so increased the carrying capacity of these cars to 44 people. (Chick Siebert.)

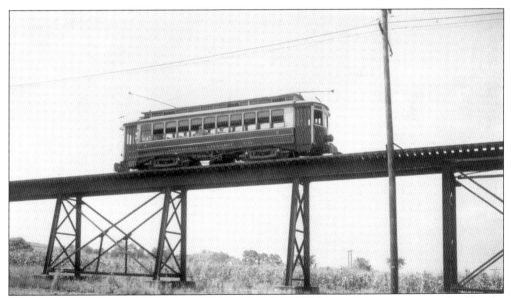

No. 2 travels across the Beverly trestle, constructed by Hershey Transit to pass over the 21-mile-long Cornwall & Lebanon Railroad. Pennsylvania Railroad purchased this line, and it became the Lebanon Branch in 1913. Much consideration was given to the addition of a third rail to Hershey Transit's wide-gauge trackage to permit the movement of standard-gauge railroad cars to and from the chocolate factory in Hershey, a proposal that was never implemented. (Neil Fasnacht collection.)

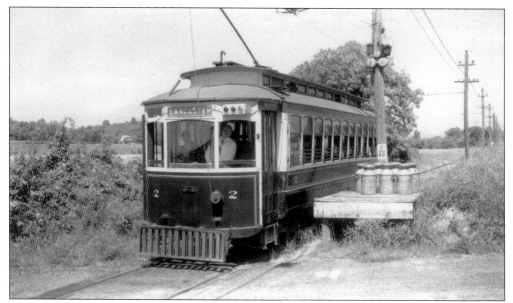

No. 2 is at the grade crossing near Shenk's Church on the Elizabethtown line, located about three fourths of a mile north of Deodate. Note the numerous milk cans sitting on the loading platform. These are just a few of the cans used to transport over 75,000 quarts of fresh milk to the chocolate factory each day. (Chick Siebert.)

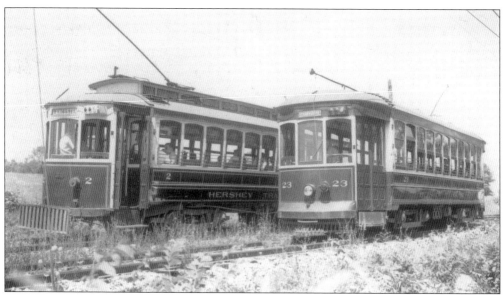

This image of No. 23 and No. 2 indicates the level of satisfaction and loyalty which the Hershey Transit had with cars produced by the J.G. Brill Company. No. 2 was part of the first order of cars placed in 1904, while No. 23, a car very similar in most aspects, was among one of the last cars to be ordered in 1915. The cars are seen as they pass one another at the siding near Shenk's Church. (Chick Siebert.)

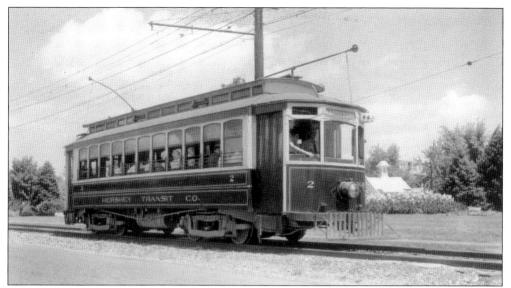

No. 2 passes in front of the old Hershey Industrial School property near the Elizabethtown and Lebanon junction during the National Railway Historical Society fan trip on August 13, 1939. (Chick Siebert.)

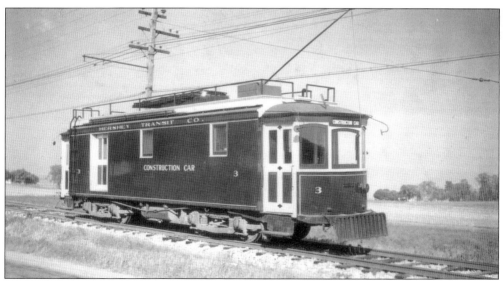

Captured here by Chick Siebert on October 19, 1939, No. 3, in its final design as the work or construction car, moves along the Elizabethtown line about a half mile south of the Ephrata Pike, near Hershey. No. 3 was equipped with Westinghouse K-6 controls, as were No. 1 and No. 2. (Chick Siebert.)

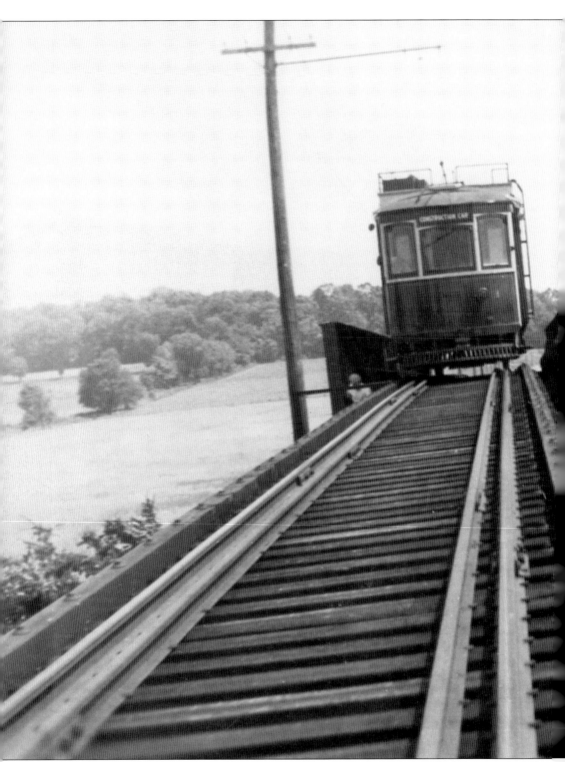

Hershey Transit was known for keeping up its property to the highest standard. Maintaining the overhead trolley wire was no exception. Construction car No. 3 is seen crossing the trestle on the

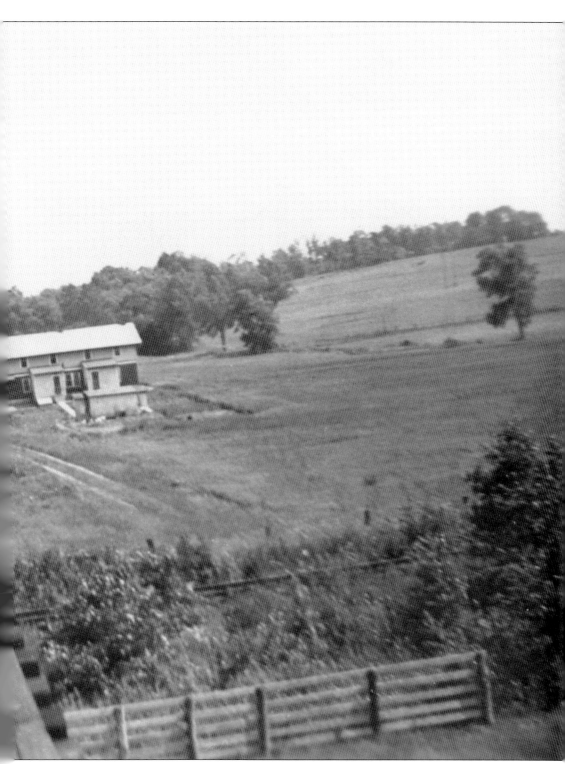

Elizabethtown line in 1938 as it travels over the system performing routine overhead wire maintenance and repair duties. (Russell Koons, Hershey Derry Township Historical Society Collection.)

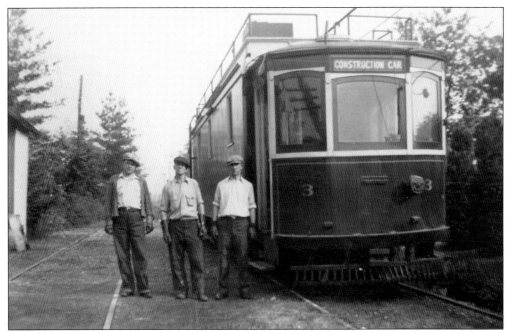

Hershey Transit construction car No. 3 is photographed here with its line crew at the terminus of the Elizabethtown line. (Russell Koons, Hershey Derry Township Historical Society Collection.)

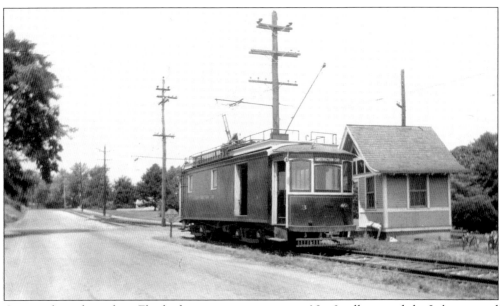

On an inbound trip from Elizabethtown, construction car No. 3 rolls toward the Lebanon and Elizabethtown junction near Homestead Lane. (Stan Bowman Jr. collection.)

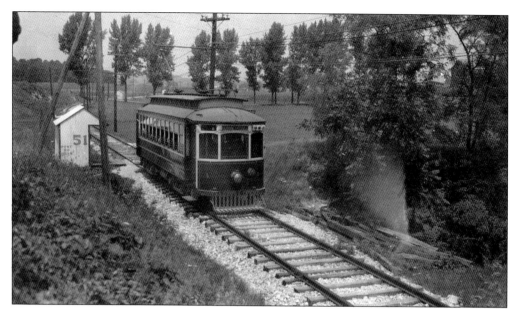

Hershey Transit No. 1, a favorite streetcar among railfans, is photographed heading south on the Elizabethtown line just south of Hershey. Shortly after service to Elizabethtown started, a proposal extend the line to Manheim, 20 miles distant, was considered to allow access to a greater number of dairies. A preliminary survey was completed by June 1916, but the line was never constructed. Perhaps wartime restrictions on materials were the cause. (Neil Fasnacht collection.)

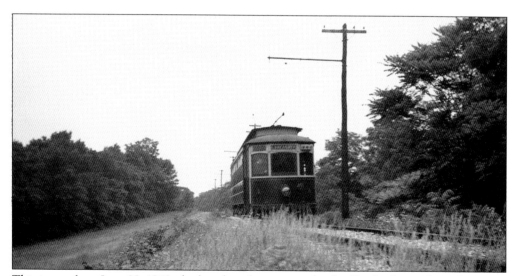

This image from June 23, 1940, the last day of operations for the Elizabethtown line, shows No. 1 dutifully carrying passengers en route to Elizabethtown, most likely for a railfan trip, as it has for many years before. (Neil Fasnacht collection.)

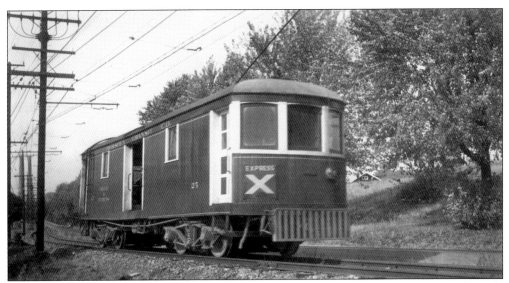

The Hershey Transit express cars, such as No. 25 (pictured here just north of Homestead Lane), visited Elizabethtown daily except Sundays to facilitate the efficient movement of carload freight and packages with the Conestoga Traction Company. As for milk, the demand for this commodity by Hershey's chocolate factory was so great that Hershey Transit not only constructed a milk station at Mount Joy, but also negotiated trackage rights to operate its own equipment over Conestoga Traction rails to provide faster service. (Dick Steinmetz, Chick Siebert collection.)

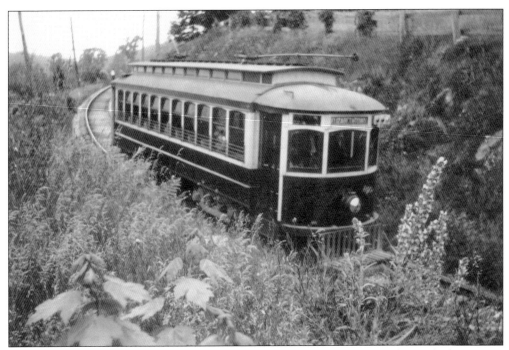

Popular among the railfan charters frequently operated over Hershey Transit during the latter years of operations, No. 1 is captured along the route to Elizabethtown. (Neil Fasnacht collection.)

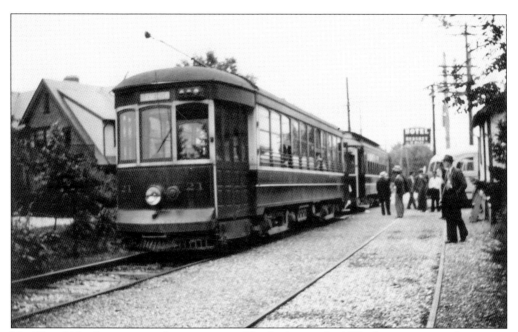

No. 21 and No. 1 are seen at the terminus in Elizabethtown. In 1932, the connecting Conestoga Traction Company converted service between Lancaster and Elizabethtown to buses. Afterwards, the Hershey Transit Company was requested to remove all of its trackage from the town's streets. A new trolley terminal was established at the town limit, and passengers were able to transfer to the bus service at this new location. Note the sign advertising the Hotel Hershey to patrons. (Neil Fasnacht collection.)

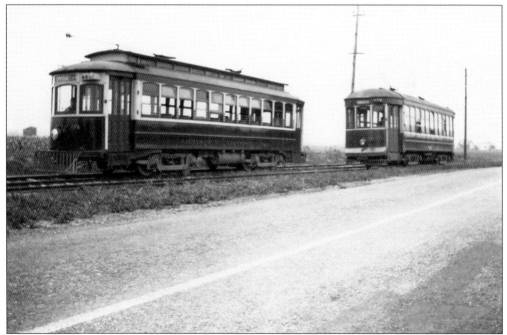

Railfans riding No. 1 and No. 16, operating as special cars on the Elizabethtown line, pass each other. Both cars were built by the J.G. Brill Company. (Neil Fasnacht collection.)

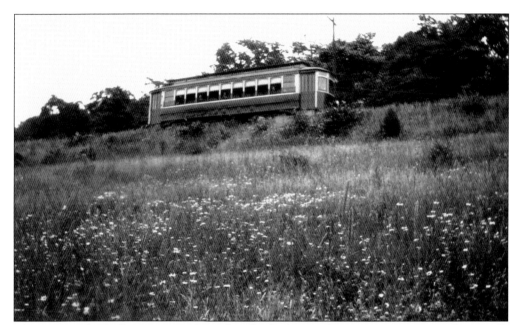

This image of a Brill car racing along the Elizabethtown line on a warm spring day recalls pleasurable memories of refreshing cool air rushing through the open windows. Located near the Elizabethtown terminal was the State Hospital for Crippled Children, created in 1930. Children destined for the hospital undoubtedly enjoyed their rides on Hershey Transit trolleys. (Neil Fasnacht collection.)

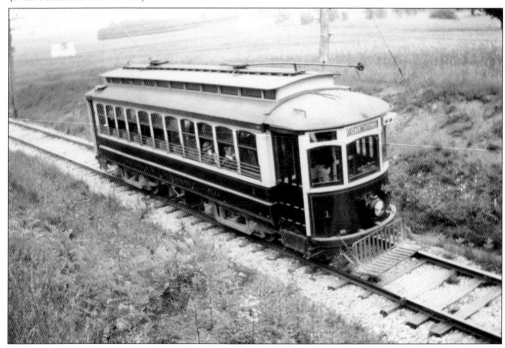

No. 1 is pictured nice and clear as a special car traveling towards its Elizabethtown destination. It is likely that this is a photograph of a charter held during the final years of operation. Service between Hershey and Elizabethtown lasted until June 23, 1940. (Neil Fasnacht collection.)

Eight

THE HOTEL LINE

Milton Hershey began construction of his hotel in 1931; however, his idea to build a hotel began 28 years prior, when he took a horse-and-buggy ride to the summit of Pat's Hill, then known as Prospect Heights. From this vantage point, he had a magnificent view to the south of the wide-open valley. On that spring day in 1903, he imagined a thriving town with a grand hotel overlooking it all.

The Hotel Line construction began in March 1913 and was completed in October of that same year. At that time, it was a rail line with no "electric" trolley service. The railway was built and serviced by a small steam locomotive. Within 18 months, the June 3, 1915, front page of the Hershey Press would report that "beginning tomorrow trolley cars will be run to the summit of the big hill overlooking Hershey." The first trolley service on the Hotel Line had begun.

With his eye on the future, Hershey constructed two 1-million gallon reservoirs at the summit, later named Highland Park, which when completed in 1916 would become the water supply for the town of Hershey and his expanding chocolate factory. In addition to transporting materials to build the reservoirs, the trolleys brought townsfolk and visitors to the summit for picnics and to enjoy the vista. Unfortunately, during the winter season, ridership declined significantly and the line was shut down through the 1920s. Around 1928 or 1929, the line was reactivated to aid in the construction of the hotel and numerous Hershey properties, including the Hershey Estates Dairy, the Park Pool & Park View Golf Club, Hershey Industrial School's Junior and Senior Hall, the Sports Arena, and the Stadium. These structures were built during a time period referred to as Milton Hershey's Great Building Campaign, and the trolleys role was of a construction workhorse as well as a mode of passenger transportation to these new and unique destinations.

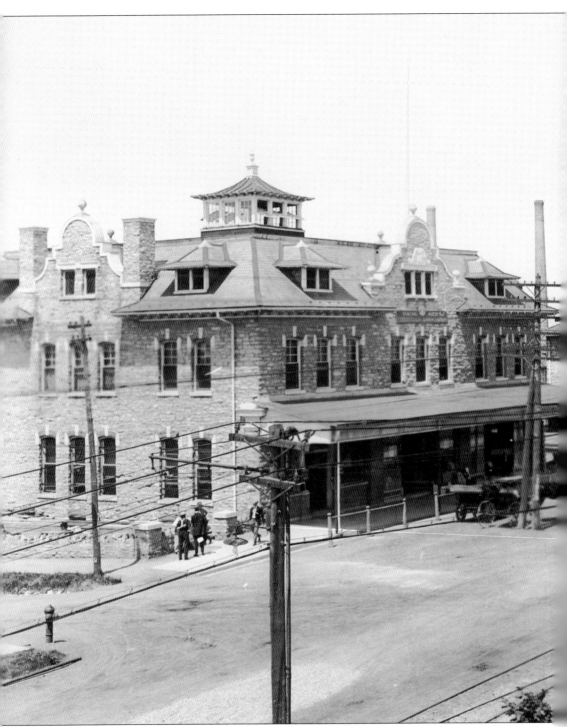

The starting point of the Hotel Line is the square in downtown Hershey. As reported in the *Hershey Press* of February 25, 1915, "a new waiting room, ticket office & superintendent's office for the Hershey Transit Co. has just opened on the first floor of the Hershey Fire Department." Its large wraparound porch hosted many patrons waiting for their trolley. Positioned in front of

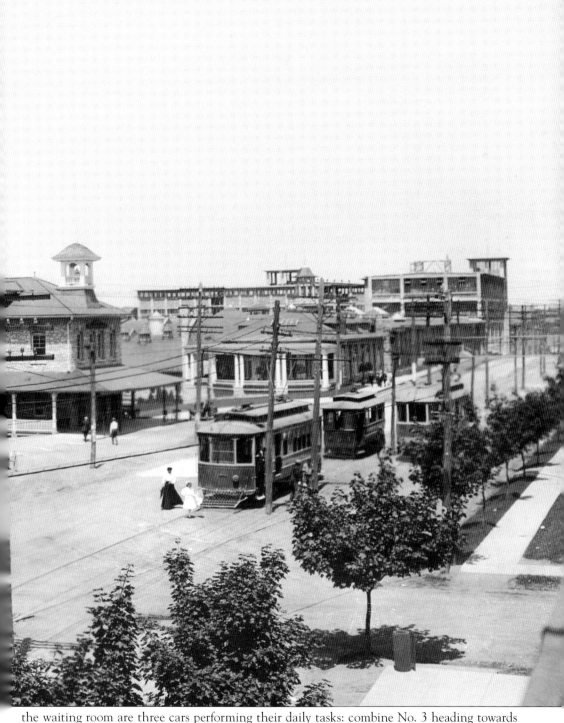

the waiting room are three cars performing their daily tasks: combine No. 3 heading towards Hummelstown, followed by No. 7, a single-truck ex-Baltimore car shuttling passengers to and from Hershey Park, and No. 9 going out on one of the six scheduled daily runs to collect milk from the dairies in Lebanon and Lancaster Counties. (Brad Ginder collection.)

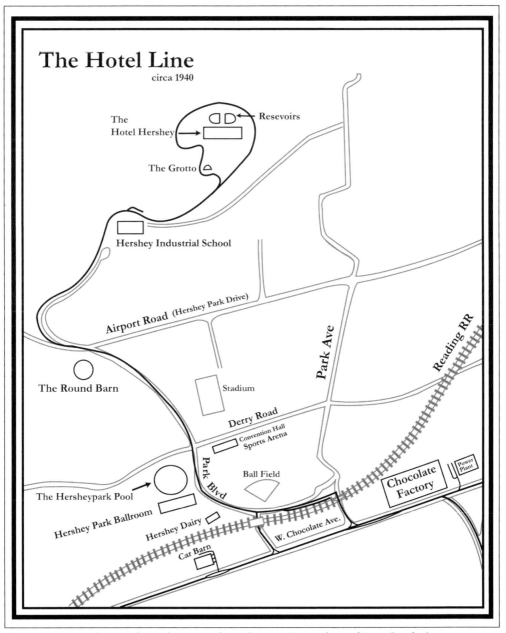

The Hotel Line

circa 1940

The
Hotel Hershey → ← Resevoirs

The Grotto

Hershey Industrial School

Airport Road (Hershey Park Drive)

The Round Barn

Stadium

Park Ave

Reading RR

Derry Road

Convention Hall
Sports Arena

Park Blvd

Ball Field

Chocolate
Factory

Power
Plant

The Hersheypark Pool →

Hershey Dairy

Hershey Park Ballroom

W. Chocolate Ave.

Car Barn

This map shows the Hotel Hershey Loop line. (Lauren Fasnacht and Lisa Ginder.)

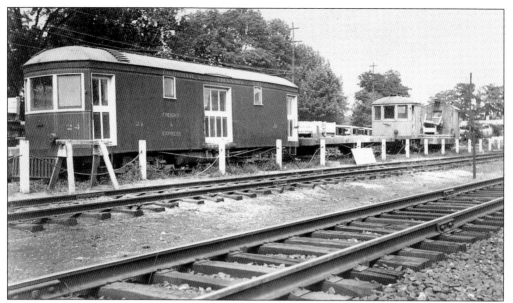

No. 24, No. 9 (rebuilt as a flatcar), and No. 28 are resting on the Hershey Park siding, which ran parallel on the north side of the Reading Railroad tracks. This siding was used extensively during the construction of the Hotel Hershey, Hershey Industrial School's Senior Hall, and the Community Center. These structures were built during the Great Depression as part of Milton Hershey's building campaign to keep residents employed. (Stan Bowman Jr. collection.)

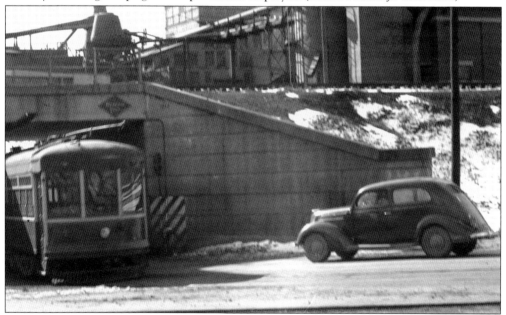

This image of No. 7 about to turn onto Park Boulevard from the Mill Street underpass shows the tight clearances that existed at this location. Clearly seen in the background is the Hershey Lumberyard. Constructed in 1914, this local landmark was unfortunately destroyed in a massive blaze on June 9, 1971. According to a 1937 Hershey Transit schedule, the travel time from the hotel to Hershey center square was 15 minutes with the trolleys clipping along at 40 miles per hour. (Neil Fasnacht collection.)

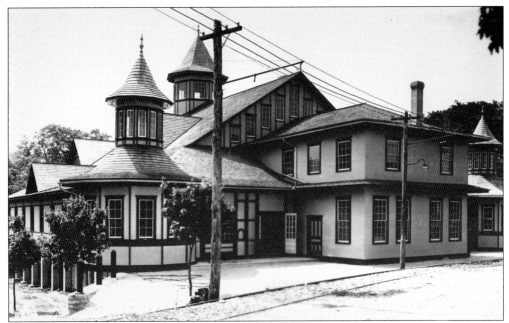

The Hershey Park Ballroom, later renamed the Starlight Ball Room (1913–1977), was a very popular place and highlighted some of America's finest bands and solo performers through the 1950s. Note the trolley tracks in the foreground. No doubt numerous couples used the trolley to arrive for their night of dancing and entertainment. The roads were unpaved at this time, so trolley travel would have been much smoother and cleaner than car or horse-drawn carriage. (Hershey Derry Township Historical Society.)

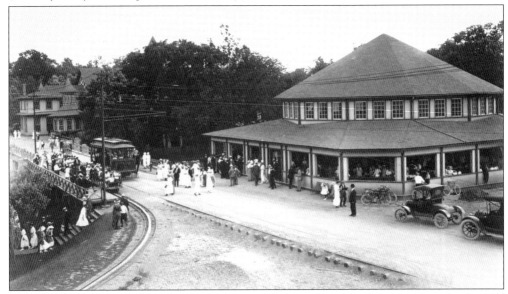

Located at the west end of Hershey Park, the second carousel was a major attraction. As pictured here in 1916, both the trolley and the park's miniature train provided an open-air ride to these very popular venues. Trolleys received their electricity from an overhead wire, whereas the miniature train employed an additional center rail to collect electricity for its motors. This third rail can easily be seen as the line curves away from the carousel. (Neil Fasnacht collection.)

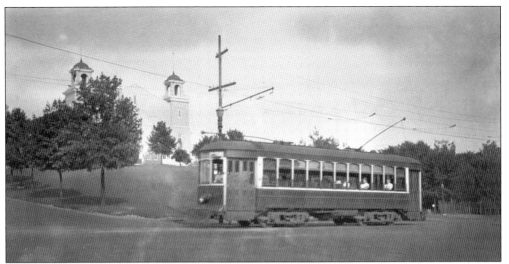

Photographed on its way to Hotel Hershey, No. 27 is shown here at the intersection of West Derry Road and Park Boulevard. The Convention Hall, also called the Ice Palace, was Hershey's first indoor skating rink until the Sports Arena was built in 1936. In 1915, work had begun on extending the line about 20 miles to Fredericksburg to meet the factory's increasing demand for additional milk, but the line was never completed. (Lisa Schirato collection.)

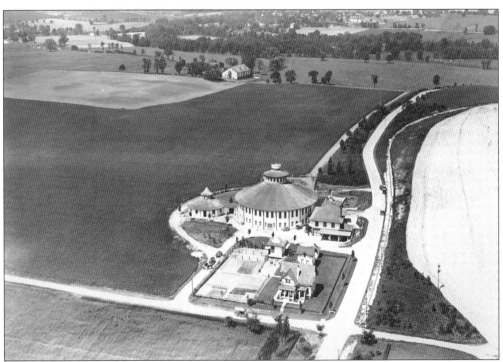

Located just north of Hershey Park, the Round Barn was Hershey's premier dairy between 1913 and 1943. The Hotel Hershey trolley line can be seen to the right of the barn. At this point, the line turned east, starting its uphill climb to the school and hotel. (Neil Fasnacht collection.)

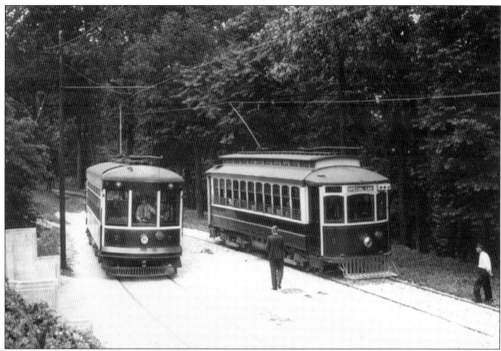

The next trolley stop along the Hotel Line was the Junior-Senior High School, which was later renamed Senior Hall. Here, No. 7 is bound for the hotel while No. 1 sits on the passing siding. No. 1 is hosting a railfan trip and is stopped for a photo opportunity, which provided many pictures for this book. (John Bowman, Hershey Derry Township Historical Society.)

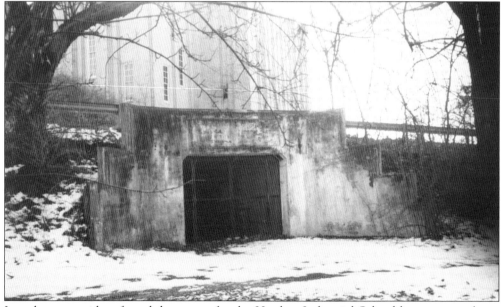

In order to provide safe and dry access for the Hershey Industrial School boys, a tunnel was constructed underneath the tracks. In this image, taken around 1990, the right-of-way was used to provide road access to a parking facility. Today, the tunnel and its entrances have been covered with earth. (Brad and Lisa Ginder.)

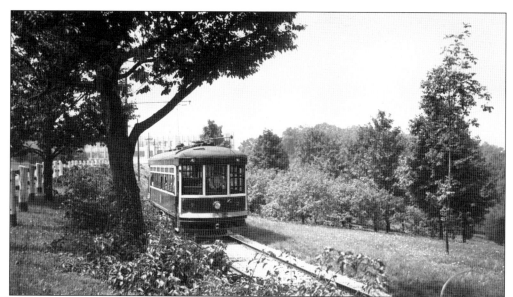

No. 7 is making the uphill climb to the Hotel Hershey just east of Senior Hall. Built for the use on that line's mountainous route, their lower gearing made these cars ideal for use on the steep grades of the Hotel Line. Because this gearing also limited their acceleration and top speed, these cars were relegated to the short runs to Palmyra, Sunday church service for the Hershey Industrial School boys, and service to the hotel. (Lisa Schirato collection.)

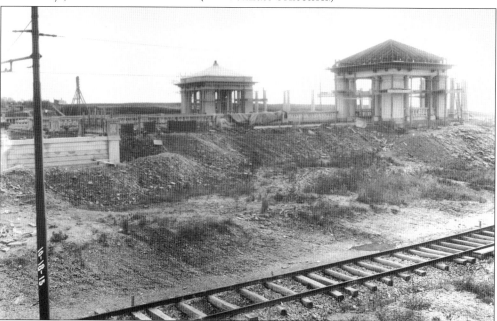

The reservoirs and pagodas are shown here under construction in October 1915 at the peak of Prospect Heights. A pump house and a filtration plant were established in the village of Sandbeach, located on Sand Creek (later renamed Manada Creek), which supplied water to these reservoirs. Initially, a small steam locomotive, or dinky, was used to build this rail line in 1913; however, as can be seen here, wires for electric trolleys indicate these reservoirs were built and serviced by trolley. (Neil Fasnacht collection.)

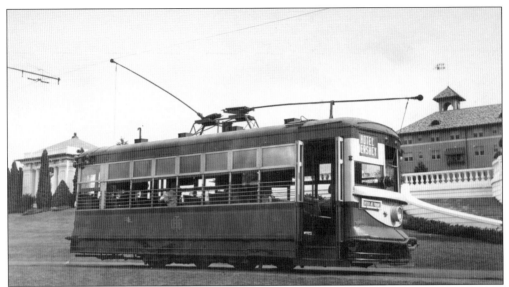

Photographed in August 1939, No. 30, known as the Birney Car, awaits passengers at the Hotel stop for its return trip to town center. This car was used extensively on this line largely for transport of Hershey Industrial School boys to Senior Hall and secondarily for Hotel Hershey guests and employees. (Neil Fasnacht collection.)

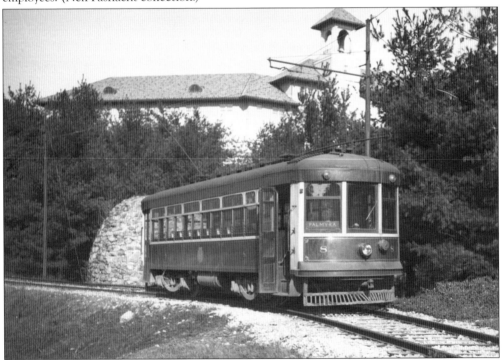

Pictured on its return trip to downtown Hershey, No. 8 passes the Grotto just to the west of the Hotel Hershey. The Grotto, or Rock Garden, was used for weddings and small group gatherings and is still a very majestic place today. This view shows the backside of the Grotto. The front is an open stage–type area surrounded by a lush flower garden built into a hillside. (Hershey Derry Township Historical Society.)

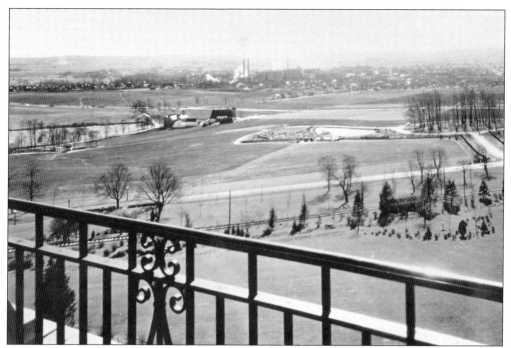

In this view looking south over the town of Hershey from the hotel balcony, the rose garden in its early stage of development dates this picture to the late 1930s. Note the trolley tracks in the foreground. This view was M.S. Hershey's vision for his town in 1903. His town and factory had indeed become a reality. (Neil Fasnacht collection.)

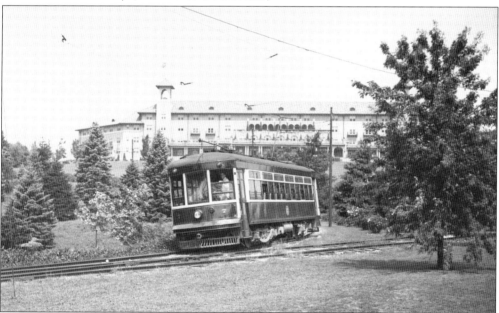

No. 7 is entering the Hotel Hershey switch on its return trip to town. The Hotel Line operated right up to December 21, 1946, the last day of the Hershey Transit Company. Many years before the construction of the Rose Garden and hotel, Milton Hershey placed 20,000 plants on this hillside for all to enjoy. (Lisa Schirato collection.)

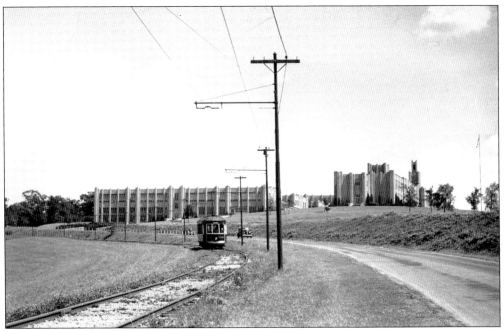

Just west of Senior Hall, No. 20 is descending the steep grade while returning to town. (Neil Fasnacht collection.)

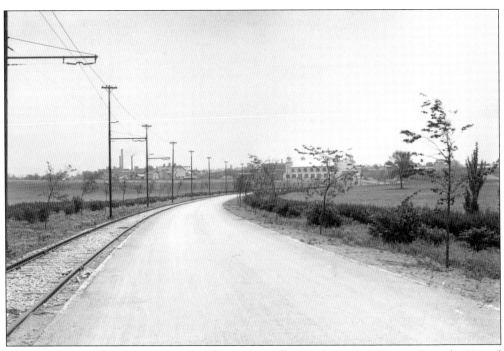

This view toward the Convention Hall shows the trolley track winding its way from the Round Barn. This road is now a tree-lined street that the Hersheypark trams uses to ferry guests to the entrance of Hersheypark. (Neil Fasnacht collection.)

Nine

ABANDONMENT

By the end of the Depression, it was clear that austere measures would have to be taken in order to permit operations to continue. Until the late 1930s, subsidies granted to the company by Hershey Estates for transporting students to and from the Hershey Industrial School and the availability of cheap electricity from the factory's power plant kept financial losses to a minimum. In an effort to prevent such losses, the company canceled its milk-hauling contract with the neighboring Lancaster, Ephrata & Lebanon Street Railway, instead preferring to permit local farmers to deliver directly to the factory by utilizing tanker trucks. To reduce payroll, cars were converted to a one-man operation.

While ridership increased substantially when the base fare was reduced to 5¢, this was offset by the fact that half the fare zones were eliminated, resulting in little revenue gains. Unfortunately, these measures were not sufficient to stem the continued losses and, as a result, the difficult decision was made to cut back service. On June 23, 1940, the Elizabethtown line was abandoned, and the Lebanon line service was cut back to Campbelltown on January 9, 1942.

However, the rising popularity of internal combustion–powered autos and trucks was also impacting the company's revenues. With this in mind, the company decided to abandon all of its lines and replace the trolley with buses. As fate would have it, the outbreak of war intervened and the seven Model 36-S buses Hershey Transit Company had ordered from the American Car & Foundry Company were diverted to Harrisburg Railways on orders from the Office of Defense Transportation, and trolleys continued their dedicated service to the community.

Following the war, trolleys found little enthusiasm for continued support from Hershey Estates. The reality of complete abandonment was difficult to avoid. After faithfully serving Hershey and the surrounding communities for nearly half a century, all remaining trolley routes were abandoned on December 21, 1946. Afterwards, the route between Palmyra and Hummelstown was replaced with bus service provided by the Hershey Coach Company, a subsidiary of the Reading Street Railway. Eventually, this service would be extended all the way into Harrisburg.

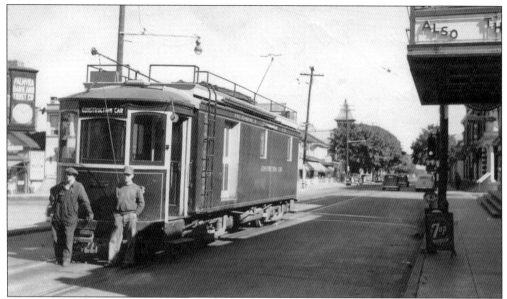

Construction car No. 3 is seen on the square in Palmyra on October 24, 1941. This car was one of the original three cars ordered by the Hummelstown & Campbellstown Street Railway. It was converted for use as a work car by the Hershey Transit shop during 1928. In this image, routine maintenance on the overhead wire is being performed. (Russell Koons, Hershey Derry Township Historical Society Collection.)

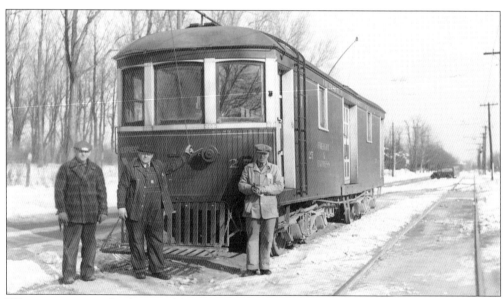

When not carrying freight to and from customers around the Hershey Transit system, No. 25 was frequently pressed into maintenance service. The crew operating the car on this day includes, from left to right, George Shirk, motorman Harry King, and Herbert Straub. This car was retired from service in 1942 following the abandonment of service between Campbelltown and Lebanon on January 9, 1942. (Russell Koons, Hershey Derry Township Historical Society Collection.)

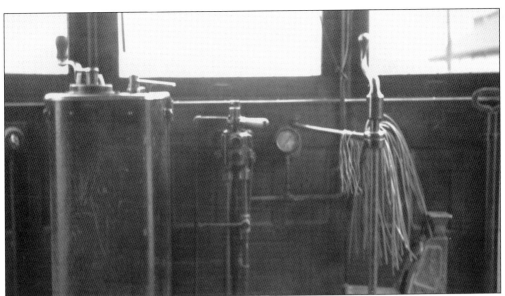

This photograph of the No. 3 cab shows the controls used by the motorman to operate the trolley. On the left is the master controller that was used to operate the motors that propelled the car. In the center of the photograph is the valve used to control the brakes. On the right is the handle for operating the car's hand brake. (Photograph by Charles Butler; Don Rhoads Jr. collection.)

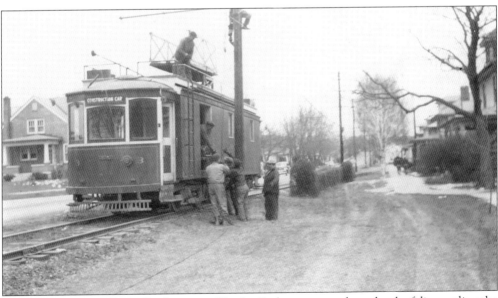

This image, captured by trolley historian Charles Butler, captures the sad task of dismantling the overhead trolley wire. The line crew, under the supervision of Russell Koons (coming down the pole), was continuing this process in Campbelltown. (Russell Koons, Hershey Derry Township Historical Society Collection.)

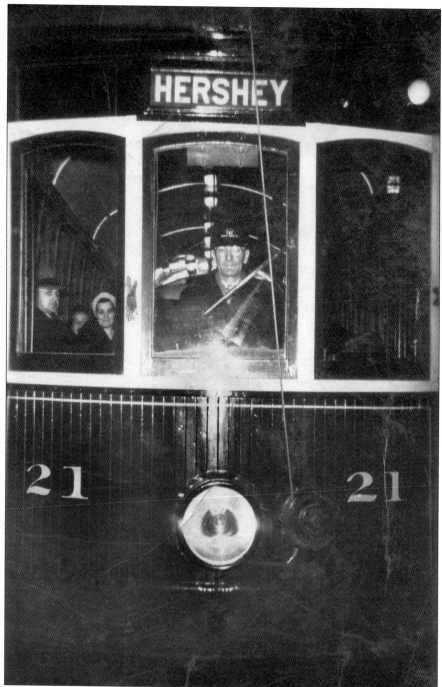

The Hershey Transit Company lasted much longer than most local trolley lines. This can be attributed to both the commitment of Milton Hershey to provide the citizens of Hershey with a safe, clean, reliable means of transportation and to the fortune of war-material shortages, which prevented the company from converting service to buses in the early 1940s. Seen here is motorman Daniel Geib at the controls one last time. (Russell Koons, Hershey Derry Township Historical Society Collection.)

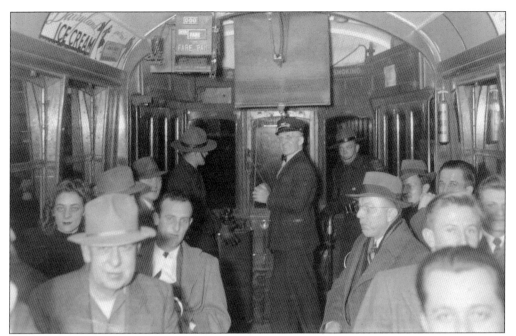

For the safety and well-being of the passengers wishing to ride on Hershey Transit trolleys one last time, two state troopers were assigned to accompany each last run on the evening of December 21, 1946. There were no reports of either mishaps or vandalism occurring that evening. (Hershey Derry Township Historical Society Collection.)

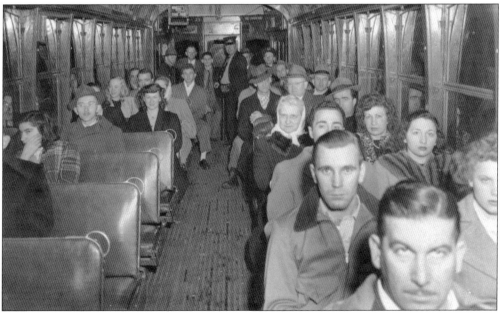

The last rides of Hershey Transit trolley operations were fully loaded with fans, well-wishers, and the local citizenry wanting to be a part of these historic events. Certainly everyone who rode the cars this night would remember fondly the friendly and reliable service the Hershey Transit Company provided the community it had faithfully served for over 42 years. (Hershey Derry Township Historical Society Collection.)

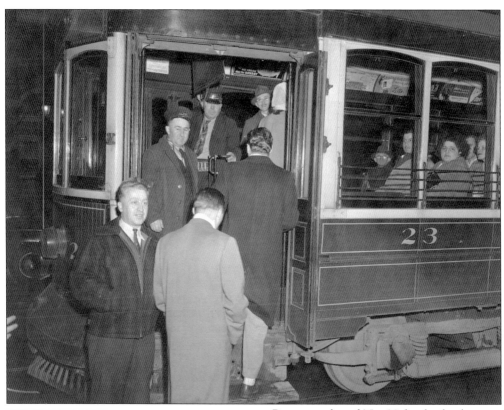

Passengers board No. 23 for the final ride to Hummelstown, where the first ride of the Hershey Transit Company predecessor, the Hummelstown & Campbellstown Street Railway, had started trolley service to Derry Church (later renamed Hershey) in 1904. (Hershey Derry Township Historical Society Collection.)

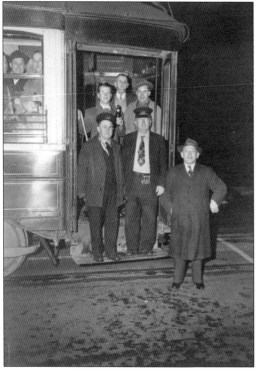

One final time, the crew members pose for a photograph before departing on their last revenue trip at midnight on December 21, 1946. (Hershey Derry Township Historical Society Collection.)

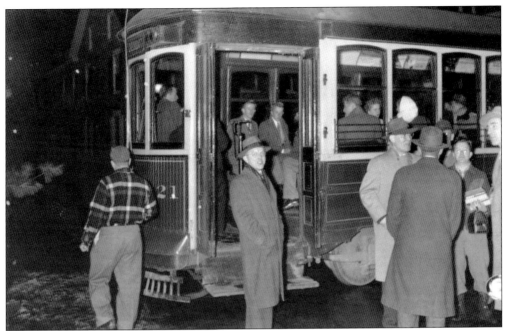

No. 21 accepts its last fare at midnight for the final run to the neighboring town of Palmyra. Once the cars completed that journey, trolley service to Hershey and the surrounding communities would come to an end. While many sadly mark the absence of their beloved trolleys, the fact remains that the overwhelming public acceptance of the automobile in deference to the reliable trolley was the primary cause of the system's demise. (Hershey Derry Township Historical Society Collection.)

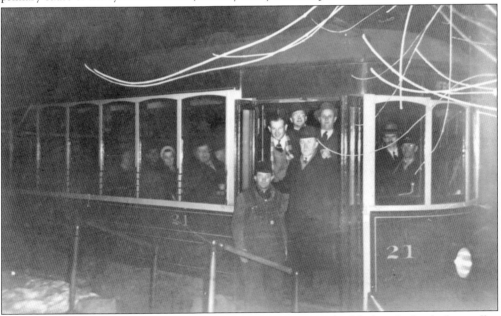

The fateful day had come for the Hershey Transit Company, as it had for hundreds of other trolley lines. Photographed by Russell Koons, for remembrance by future generations, is No. 21 making the last trip to Palmyra under the watchful eye of motorman Owen Hughes at midnight on December 21, 1946. (Russell Koons, Hershey Derry Township Historical Society Collection.)

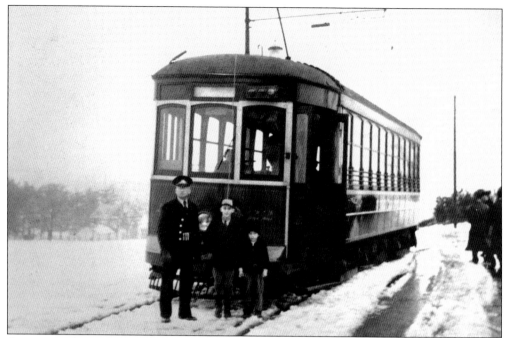

On a wet and snowy day in 1946, No. 22 is pictured with motorman and conductor John Cassell at the Hotel Hershey. It is likely this photograph was taken on the last day of service. Cassell also ran the last run to Campbelltown with this car. One of the many incredibly reliable and durable semi-convertible cars Hershey Transit had purchased from the J.G. Brill Company, No. 22 was purchased in 1915 and served the community for over 30 years. (Photograph by Charles Butler; Neil Fasnacht collection.)

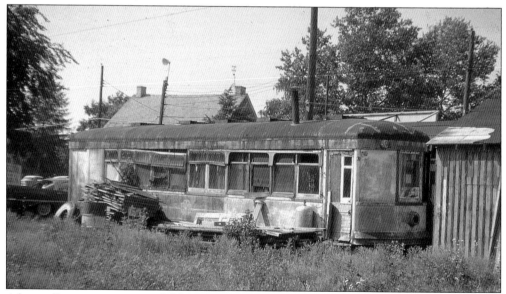

After trolley operations ceased, No. 4 was put up for sale in 1947 for the sum of $450. Records indicate that all equipment had been removed from the car prior to being offered. No. 4 ended up in Harrisburg and was remodeled for use as a fruit and vegetable stand, as pictured here. (Lisa Schirato collection.)

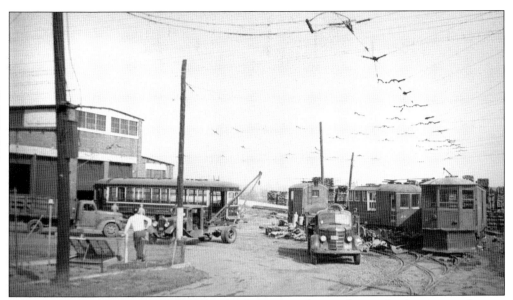

Following their abandonment, the sad task of scrapping the cars began. In this image taken on April 30, 1947, No. 19 is being stripped of all parts prior to being scrapped. Not only were the cars salvaged, but so was almost all of the track and the overhead wire. Notice the numerous stacks of salvaged ties in the background of the photograph. (Neil Fasnacht collection.)

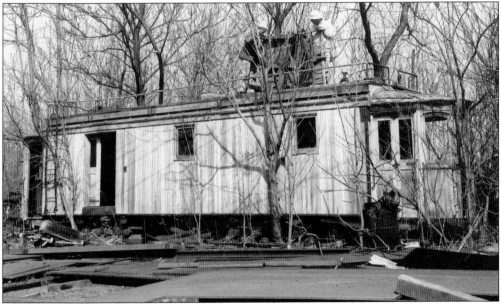

No. 3 had the longest operating career with the Hershey Transit Company. Delivered as a combine and used to carry passengers and freight, No. 3 inaugurated trolley service for the Hummelstown & Campbellstown Street Railway. The car was later converted to a straight passenger coach. When additional maintenance equipment was necessary, No. 3 was converted again, this time into a construction car in 1928. Following the abandonment of trolley service in December 1946, the car was used to remove overhead wire and rails. Pictured in this photograph, No. 3 was sold to Wolf's Salvage Yard in nearby Hummelstown for final disposition. (Rockhill Trolley Museum Collection.)

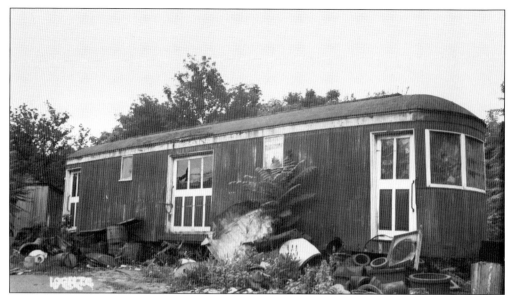

After assisting construction car No. 3 with the dismantling of the rails and overhead wire, express motor No. 24 has met the same fate, languishing in Wolf's Salvage Yard with the unlikely prospect of ever turning a wheel again. This was, unfortunately, a very common fate for the trolleys that reliably moved people and freight during the first half of the 20th century. (Neil Fasnacht collection.)

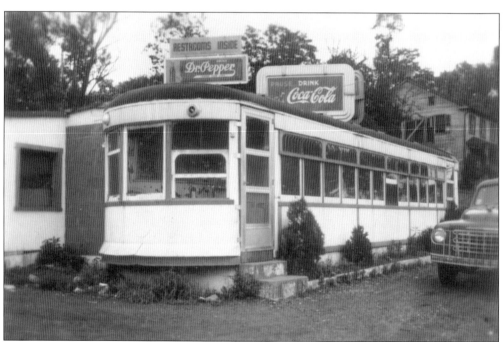

One of the former Ephrata & Lebanon cars, No. 8 is seen here in Highspire, Pennsylvania, being used as a diner in 1949. It was common to use old trolleys as homes, cabins, chicken coops, and sheds as they were easy to transport and available at a very reasonable cost. To this day, from time to time, old trolleys are still discovered after many years. (Elmer Fry, Chick Siebert collection.)

Ten

FRIENDS OF THE

HERSHEY TROLLEY

In 1995, Friends of the Hershey Trolley (FOHT), under the auspices of the Derry Township Historical Society and leadership of Brad and Lisa Ginder, was formed with the mission of education and preservation of the Hershey Transit trolley system. Through the tireless efforts of many dedicated volunteers and with the assistance of other trolley preservation groups, FOHT has been able to locate and return to Hershey two of the cars that once ran along Chocolate Avenue.

Built by the J.G. Brill Company, and one of the first three cars ordered, No. 3 was one of two combination cars, carrying passengers and freight. During the mid-1920s, the car was converted to an all-passenger car. In 1928, No. 3 was transformed into a construction car, carrying maintenance men and tools. After trolley service ended in 1946, No. 3 remained in operation until 1948 to perform the task of removing the overhead wires and pulling up the rails.

With No. 3's work completed, the trolley was sold to Wolf's Salvage Yard in Hummelstown. In 1967, it was purchased by a trolley museum in New Jersey. By 2005, it was owned by Railways to Yesterday, also known as the Rockhill Trolley Museum. On April 22, 2006, Rockhill transferred ownership of Hershey No. 3 to the Derry Township Historical Society.

No. 7 was built by the Cincinnati Car Company in 1914 for the Ephrata & Lebanon traction line and ran as No. 21 until 1931. No. 21 was sold to Hershey Transit, along with Nos. 20 and 30; the cars were refurbished and put into use as Nos. 4, 7, and 8 in 1934. The three Cincinnati cars ran until the end in 1946. In 2007, FOHT acquired No. 7 from Amy Dolbin, who was using the streetcar as her residence in Enola, Pennsylvania. The car had been converted into a residence in the 1940s by Amy's grandparents, Pearl and Roy Gouffer, after Hershey Transit ceased to exist. No. 7 was returned to Hershey on Tuesday, August 28, 2007, and is currently stored in the West Car Barn, along with No. 3. Both streetcars are awaiting restoration to operable service.

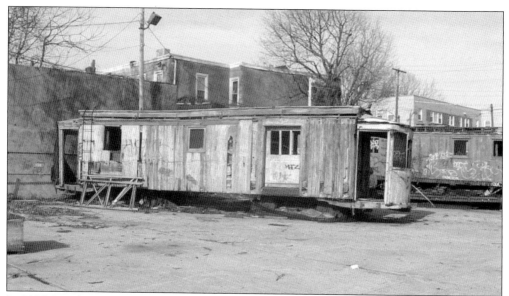

In 2006, Hershey Transit No. 3 was donated to the Friends of the Hershey Trolley, a committee of the Hershey Derry Township Historical Society, from Railways to Yesterday, also known as the Rockhill Trolley Museum. Here, on February 24, 2006, No. 3 awaits plans for its future in a SEPTA depot in Germantown, Philadelphia. (Lisa Schirato.)

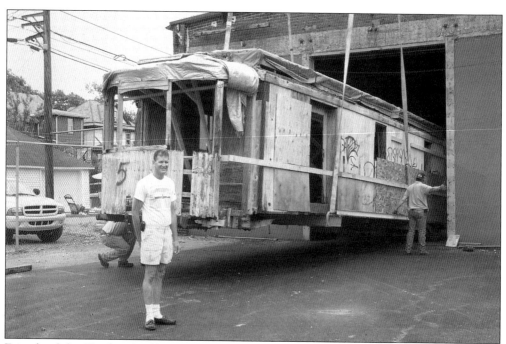

Friends of the Hershey Trolley volunteer Brad Ginder stands in front of work car No. 3 as Pete Davis, of First Davis Corporation, with the help of a crane and his crew, gently eases No. 3 into the southernmost track bay, on the east end of the West Car Barn, on June 7, 2006. (Lisa Schirato.)

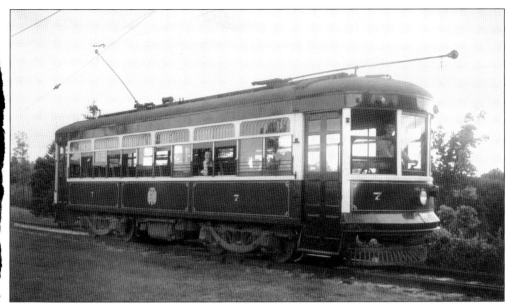

No. 7 is pictured here on the Hotel Hershey line in 1939. Note the pristine condition of the car. The Hershey Transit Company was known for the meticulous upkeep of its trolleys. One of the goals of FOHT is to restore No. 7 to operating condition and provide the public with the opportunity to once again take a ride on a Hershey Transit trolley. (Chick Siebert.)

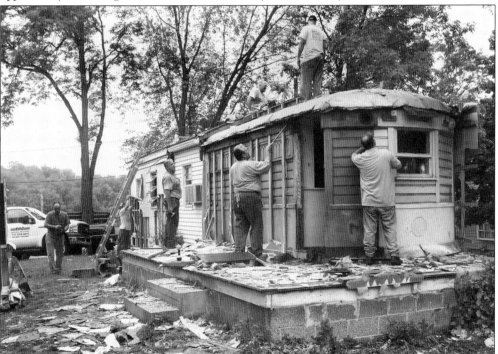

Volunteers from the Milton Hershey School, the Purcell Company, and Friends of the Hershey Trolley work together uncovering Hershey No. 7 in Enola on August 25, 2007. Visible are two sections of the decorative leaded-glass windows that were prominent on this car, produced originally for the Ephrata & Lebanon Traction Company by the Cincinnati Car Company. (Lisa Schirato.)

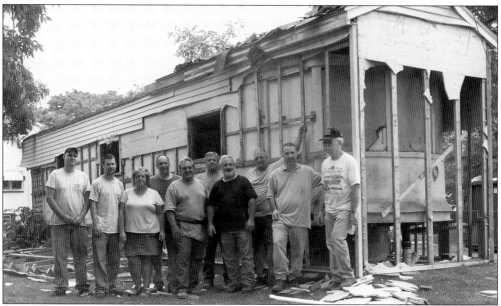

After Hershey Transit stopped operating, Hershey No. 7, originally Ephrata & Lebanon No. 21, was used as a home from the 1940s to 2007. When first purchased, the car was placed on top of a hand-dug basement and lived in as is. During the 1960s, a contractor was hired to cover the trolley with aluminum siding and a roof, converting the streetcar into a "real" home. Pictured are volunteers at end of demolition workday, August 25, 2007. (Lisa Schirato.)

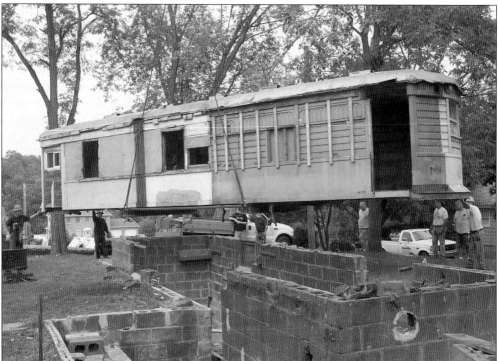

An exciting but tense moment is pictured here as Hershey No. 7 is lifted off its house foundation on Dauphin Street in Enola, Pennsylvania, on August 28, 2007. (Lisa Schirato.)

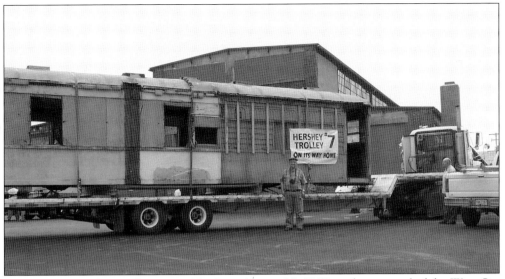

Tod Prowell stands proudly next to No. 7 on August 28, 2007, at the east end of the West Car Barn on the day the car returned home to Hershey from Enola, Pennsylvania, where it had been used as a house since the late 1940s. (Lisa Schirato.)

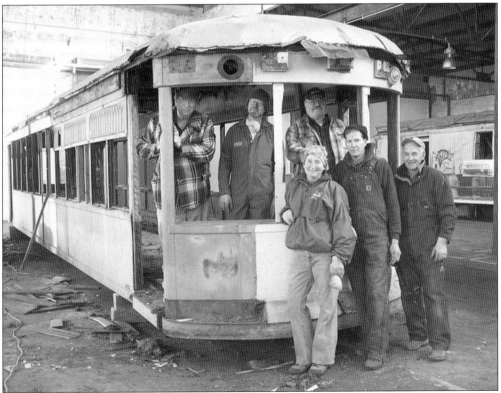

Friends of the Hershey Trolley volunteers, from left to right, (first row) Lisa Ginder, Brad Ginder, and Don Fasnacht; (second row) Richard Rissmiller, Tim Abbott, and Jim Behrens work on removing the last remains of the house exterior material from No. 7 in the West Car Barn on January 1, 2008. (Lisa Schirato.)

DISCOVER THOUSANDS OF LOCAL HISTORY BOOKS
FEATURING MILLIONS OF VINTAGE IMAGES

Arcadia Publishing, the leading local history publisher in the United States, is committed to making history accessible and meaningful through publishing books that celebrate and preserve the heritage of America's people and places.

Find more books like this at
www.arcadiapublishing.com

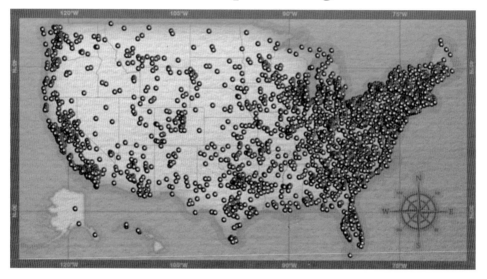

Search for your hometown history, your old stomping grounds, and even your favorite sports team.

Consistent with our mission to preserve history on a local level, this book was printed in South Carolina on American-made paper and manufactured entirely in the United States. Products carrying the accredited Forest Stewardship Council (FSC) label are printed on 100 percent FSC-certified paper.

MADE IN THE
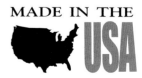
USA